Contents

Features

PROCESSOR POWER℠: SEAFOOD MOUSSELINES

2 Mousselines, those light and airy French creations that were once laborious and time-consuming to prepare, may now be made easily and speedily in a food processor. Our mousseline recipes feature two handsome Seafood Terrines and a fascinating Seafood Delice.

SOUTHWESTERN PASTA— COOL & HOT
by Anne Lindsay Greer

9 A processor expert has enlivened Southwestern cuisine by creating two new kinds of fettuccine— one flavored with jalapeño and one with red chili—to use in salads and hot dishes.

HOME WEDDING BUFFET
by Abby Mandel

14 Our Contributing Editor re-creates her summer wedding buffet. Following her timetable, home cooks can make this buffet for fifty—including a delicious three-tier cake—with assurance.

PROCESSOR EASE: POUND CAKE

24 Good News: a new processor recipe for a delicious light pound cake and five outstanding variations of it.

A TOUCH OF SAFFRON
by Nika Hazelton

27 Saffron is not to be used with abandon. A pinch brilliantly colors and subtly flavors a wide range of dishes, from an iced soup to a famous Pennsylvania-Dutch coffee cake.

A FRENCH CHEF COOKS DINNER

34 Jean Berrard, a classically trained French chef, visited THE PLEASURES OF COOKING kitchen and prepared a delightful dinner that cooks everywhere can duplicate.

GUATEMALAN BRUNCH
by Copeland Marks

40 A cooking teacher and world traveler offers an array of interesting dishes, each complementing the other, to vary that all-American pastime: brunch.

Departments

A COOKBOOK SAMPLER

46 Richard Sax, a young and talented cooking teacher, has written a fine book full of useful recipes, *Cooking Great Meals Every Day*. From it we present two desserts: Almond Brittle Cookies and Homemade Double Chocolate Pudding.

SHARING RECIPES

48 A reader contributes a lovely Lime Almond Tart.

49 RECIPE INDEX

Seafood Mousselines

*M*ousselines—airy combinations of minced seafood, veal or poultry plus egg white and cream—are one of the finest inventions of France's haute cuisine.

Susan Smith, a member of our staff—under the guidance of Carl Sontheimer, our publisher—recently embarked on a three-month mousseline marathon, testing countless seafood combinations. The numerous combinations were then narrowed down to two recipes for mousselines, both delectable and dependable, and both made in a food processor. Also worked out were three innovative ways of using the two mousselines in a Seafood Delice and in two Seafood Terrines. Recipes for these delightful dishes follow.

*I*n classic French cuisine, making mousselines necessitated long and tiring physical effort. The seafood, veal or poultry had to be ground by hand, chilled, forced through the extremely fine mesh of a sieve and seasoned. Then the mixture had to be beaten over ice as egg white was slowly added. Next the cook gradually incorporated chilled cream, never allowing the beating arm to falter for a moment.

If any step was hurried, if the mixture or the cream was insufficiently chilled, the result was an oily, semi-fluid paste. Fortunately the processor has eliminated these laborious hand steps. Moreover, the processor is especially useful in making seafood mousselines because it not only chops and mixes with extraordinary speed, but eliminates sieving.

Seafood Terrines are served in the form of rings, a pretty and practical presentation. The Seafood Delice is unusually imaginative. Its development was inspired by an experience of Carl Sontheimer's.

In 1961 he dined at the three-star

Processor Power^{SM}— *introducing innovative techniques in food processor cookery— appears periodically.*

Clockwise from below: Seafood Delices made with Shrimp and Scallop Mousseline, Seafood Delices made with Cod and Scallop Mousseline with Spinach, and Seafood Delices made with Cod and Scallop Mousseline; all served with shrimp sauce.

Auberge de Noves, an inn and restaurant near Avignon, France. The owner, Monsieur Lalleman, served what might be called seafood mousseline "pancakes," sparsely filled and surrounded with a flavorful sauce. Monsieur Lalleman talked freely about the difficulty of their preparation.

"I am proud of them," he said. "They are not easy to make. I am sure, Monsieur, that you are a good enough cook to know that the first four times you attempt them, you will fail."

Needless to say, they were the products of arduous hand work. By using our processor recipe, you can succeed the first time you make them. And you can keep them on hand in your freezer. Baked and sealed in an airtight wrapping, they will stay frozen for up to three months. To use, defrost them in the refrigerator, unwrap, fill, and bake at 350°F. for 20 minutes before serving with their sauce.— L.S.

Note: If your food processor has a work bowl with an inside width greater than 6 1/2 inches, you can process all quantities given for each mousseline recipe in a single batch.

SHRIMP AND SCALLOP MOUSSELINE

Be sure to reserve the shrimp shells. They will be needed for the sauce accompanying Seafood Delices, or for Terrine Sauce for Seafood Terrine with Leek and Fennel. Shrimp shells freeze well: wrap them securely in aluminum foil, then in plastic wrap.

> 1 pound medium shrimp, peeled and deveined
> ¾ pound sea scallops, rinsed and patted dry
> 1½ teaspoons salt
> ½ teaspoon Tabasco
> ½ teaspoon freshly grated nutmeg
> 2 large egg whites, in separate measures
> 2½ cups heavy cream

Use the metal blade of a food processor to process half of the shrimp with half of the scallops, ¾ teaspoon of the salt, ¼ teaspoon Tabasco and ¼ teaspoon nutmeg until very smooth, at least 90 seconds. Stop 3 times to scrape down the bowl.

With the machine running, add 1 of the egg whites and 1¼ cups of the cream through the feed tube and process until well blended, at least 15 seconds. Stop and scrape the bowl once. The mixture should be thick and fluffy. Transfer to a 2-quart mixing bowl.

Repeat with the remaining ingredients, and with a spatula gently fold the mixtures together in the mixing bowl.

The mousseline can be refrigerated, well covered, for 1 day. It can be frozen for up to 3 months.

Makes 1 recipe, about 6 cups.

COD AND SCALLOP MOUSSELINE

> ¾ pound cod fillets, cut into 2-inch pieces
> ¾ pound sea scallops, rinsed and patted dry
> 1½ teaspoons salt
> ½ teaspoon Tabasco
> ½ teaspoon freshly grated nutmeg
> 2 large egg whites, in separate measures
> 2½ cups heavy cream

Use the metal blade of a food processor to process half of the cod with half of the scallops, ¾ teaspoon of the salt, ¼ teaspoon Tabasco and ¼ teaspoon nutmeg until very smooth, at least 90 seconds. Stop 3 times to scrape down the bowl.

With the machine running, add 1 of the egg whites and 1¼ cups of the cream through the feed tube and process until well blended, at least 15 seconds. Stop to scrape the bowl once. The mixture should be thick and fluffy. Transfer to a 2-quart mixing bowl.

Repeat with the remaining ingredients, and with a spatula gently fold the mixtures together in the mixing bowl.

The mousseline can be refrigerated, well covered, for 1 day. It can be frozen for up to 3 months.

Makes 1 recipe, about 6 cups.

Variations:
The addition of carrot or spinach does not alter the flavor of the Cod and Scallop Mousseline but does give it a distinct color.

Cod and Scallop Mousseline with Carrot
Trim and peel a small carrot. Cut into ¼-inch slices and cook in simmering, salted water for 30 minutes or until very soft. Drain well. Process half of the carrot slices with each batch of cod and scallops.

Cod and Scallop Mousseline with Spinach
Stem and wash 10 large spinach leaves (about 4 ounces). In a 1½-quart saucepan, bring ¼ cup of water to a boil. Add the spinach, cover and cook over low heat for about 5 minutes or until wilted and soft. Immediately run the spinach under cold running water. Drain and squeeze between the palms of your hands to remove as much moisture as possible. Process half of the spinach with each batch of the cod and scallops.

SEAFOOD DELICES WITH SHRIMP SAUCE

Each delice is a thin 5-inch circle of mousseline mixture. Golden caviar is an American product, the roe of whitefish from the Great Lakes. It is much less expensive than sturgeon caviar, and it freezes well. Good fish markets and gourmet stores carry it.

½ recipe Shrimp and Scallop Mousseline (recipe on page 4) (see NOTE, page 6)
½ pound medium shrimp, unshelled
1½ cups dry white wine
1 cup water
1 large shallot, peeled and halved
½ pound mushrooms, cleaned, with ends trimmed
4 tablespoons (½ stick) unsalted butter
1 tablespoon vegetable oil
Salt
Freshly ground black pepper
4 ounces golden caviar
2 tablespoons unbleached all-purpose flour
⅛ teaspoon freshly ground white pepper
Pinch freshly grated nutmeg
½ cup heavy cream

Making the Delices:

Preheat the oven to 200°F.

Line two 17- by 14-inch cookie sheets with wax paper. Use a 5-inch plate as a guide, or cut out a cardboard circle, and with the point of a knife gently trace 6 circles on each sheet of the wax paper (fig. 1), being careful not to cut through the wax paper. Butter the wax paper.

Fill a pastry bag fitted with a ¼-inch plain tip with ⅓ of the mousseline. Pipe an outline of each circle (fig. 2). Using the back of a small spoon, spread the mixture toward the center. Divide the remaining mousseline evenly among the delices and spread the mixture to fill in each circle (fig. 3). Each delice should be about ⅛-inch thick. Butter wax paper and place buttered side down over the delices.

Bake in the center of the preheated oven for 20 minutes or until set. Carefully pull away the top sheets of wax paper. Run a knife under the edge of the delices and gently peel away from the wax paper. Set aside between sheets of wax paper.

(At this point the delices may be refrigerated, well wrapped, for up to 1 day; or frozen, sealed in an airtight wrapping, for up to 3 months.)

Making the Filling:

Peel and devein the shrimp, reserving the shells. (Add the reserved shrimp shells from the Shrimp and Scallop Mousseline recipe.) In a 1½-quart saucepan bring the shrimp shells, wine and water to a boil. Reduce the heat and simmer gently, uncovered, for 30 minutes.

Strain the shrimp stock into a mixing bowl; let the sediment settle to the bottom. Rinse and wipe out the saucepan and return the clear stock to the pan, discarding the sediment.

Bring the stock to a simmer. Add the reserved shrimp and cook for 2 minutes or until just cooked through. With a slotted spoon remove the shrimp. Strain the stock through several layers of rinsed cheesecloth into a small mixing bowl and set aside for the sauce.

Use the metal blade of a food processor to chop the shrimp, pulsing until finely chopped. Set aside in a 1-quart mixing bowl.

With the machine running drop the shallot through the feed tube and process until minced. Add the mushrooms and pulse 2 or 3 times and then process for about 5 seconds or until the mushrooms are finely chopped. Stop once to scrape the bowl.

Heat 2 tablespoons of the butter with the oil in a medium skillet over moderate heat. Add the mushroom mixture and cook, stirring often, until the liquid has evaporated and the mushrooms are lightly browned, about 10 minutes. Add salt and freshly ground black pepper to taste. Add to the chopped shrimp and stir to mix.

Assembling the Delices and Finishing the Sauce:

Preheat the oven to 350°F. Butter a 13- by 9- by 2-inch baking pan and set aside.

Spread 1 rounded tablespoon of the shrimp and mushroom mixture evenly over half of each delice (fig. 4). Spread ½ teaspoon of caviar over the mushroom mixture and fold the other half of the delice over the filling.

Place the delices in a single layer, overlapping slightly, in the prepared pan and cover tightly with aluminum foil. Bake in the center of the preheated oven for 20 minutes or until heated through.

Meanwhile, heat the remaining 2 tablespoons of butter in a 1-quart saucepan over low heat. Stir in the flour and cook for 1 minute. Slowly add the reserved

1. Tracing a 5-inch circle.   2. Piping an outline.   3. Spreading the mousseline.   4. Spreading mushroom mixture over ½ of the delice.

shrimp stock, ¼ teaspoon of salt, the freshly ground white pepper and nutmeg and cook over moderate heat, stirring, until the sauce is smooth and has thickened slightly, about 5 minutes. Cover and set aside.

Presentation:

Just before serving, stir ¼ cup of the cream into the sauce and heat through over low heat. (If the sauce is too thick, add cream by tablespoons until the desired consistency is reached.) Place 2 delices on each serving plate and divide the sauce evenly among them. Garnish with the remaining caviar.

Makes 6 first course or luncheon servings. NOTE: The delices may be made with Cod and Scallop Mousseline. In that case, make the stock using the shells from the ½ pound of shrimp called for in the filling.

SEAFOOD TERRINE WITH LEEK AND FENNEL

1 medium fennel bulb, stalks removed (about 7 ounces), tough outer layers removed, quartered, cored and cleaned
1 large leek (about 7 ounces), trimmed, split, cleaned and cut to fit feed tube vertically
1 tablespoon unsalted butter
  Salt and freshly ground black pepper
  Vegetable oil for pan
  Carrot slices, thinly sliced, for garnish (optional)
  Tomato skin, for garnish (optional)
  Fennel fronds or fresh dill, for garnish (optional)
1 recipe Shrimp and Scallop Mousseline (recipe on page 4)
  Terrine Sauce (recipe follows)

Use the metal blade of a food processor to chop the fennel until finely chopped. Insert the medium slicing disc and process the leek.

Heat the butter in a medium skillet over moderately low heat. Add the fennel and leek and cook, stirring occasionally, until they are soft but not browned, about 8 minutes. Add salt and pepper to taste. Transfer to a mixing bowl and set aside. (You should have about 1 cup.)

Preheat the oven to 250°F. and oil a 4½-cup ring mold.

Arrange carrot slices, pieces of tomato skin and fennel fronds (if used) in the bottom of the prepared mold, making a decorative pattern (for technique, see fig. 1, page 8).

Use ½ of the mousseline to line the inside of the mold with a ½-inch layer (fig. 2), smoothing to eliminate air bubbles.

Gently fold ½ of the remaining mousseline into the reserved cooked vegetables. Then spoon the mixture into the lined mold, smoothing the top of the vegetables (fig. 3).

Put the remaining mousseline into a pastry bag fitted with a ½-inch plain tip. Pipe the mousseline over the vegetable mixture to cover (fig 4). Smooth the top. Tap the mold on a counter several times to release air bubbles. Place the mold on a baking sheet and bake in the center of the preheated oven for 55 to 60 minutes or until the internal temperature reaches 155°F.

Meanwhile, 15 minutes before removing the terrine from the oven prepare the Terrine Sauce.

Remove the mold to a wire rack and let cool for 10 to 15 minutes. Run a knife around both edges of the mold; then place a serving platter over the mold and invert.

To serve, spoon some of the Terrine Sauce onto a plate and arrange two slices of the terrine on it, or serve the sauce separately.

Serves 12 to 16.

Terrine Sauce

  Shells from 1 pound medium shrimp, reserved from the Shrimp and Scallop Mousseline preparation (recipe on page 4), defrosted if frozen
2 cups dry white wine
1¼ cups water
3 tablespoons unsalted butter
3 tablespoons flour
¼ teaspoon salt
⅛ teaspoon freshly ground white pepper
3 drops Tabasco
  Pinch freshly grated nutmeg
¾ cup heavy cream

In a 1½-quart saucepan, bring the shrimp shells, the wine and water to a boil. Reduce the heat and simmer gently, uncovered, for 30 minutes.

Strain the shrimp stock into a mixing bowl; let the sediment settle to the bottom. Carefully ladle the stock through several layers of rinsed cheesecloth into a small mixing bowl, avoiding the sediment. Set aside.

Heat the butter in a 1½-quart saucepan over low heat. Stir in the flour and cook for 1 minute. Slowly add the reserved shrimp stock, salt, pepper, Tabasco and nutmeg and cook over moderate heat, stirring, until the sauce is smooth and has thickened slightly, about 5 minutes. Cover and set aside.

Just before serving, stir ½ cup of the cream into the sauce and heat through over low heat. (If the sauce is too thick, add cream by tablespoons until the desired consistency is reached.)

Makes about 2 cups.

Seafood Terrine with Leek and Fennel, served with Terrine Sauce.

SEAFOOD TERRINE WITH RED PEPPER AND SCALLIONS

1 large sweet red pepper (about 6 ounces)
2 bunches medium scallions (about 6 ounces)
  Vegetable oil for pan
  Carrot slices, thinly sliced, for garnish (optional)
1 recipe Cod and Scallop Mousseline with
  Carrot (recipe on page 4); do not use the spinach
  variation
  White Wine Sauce (recipe follows)

Core, seed and quarter the red pepper. Set aside a ½-inch square for garnish. Use the metal blade of a food processor to chop the red pepper, pulsing 6 to 8 times.

Trim the scallions of all but 2-inches of green, reserving some of the green for garnish. Cut the scallions to fit the feed tube vertically. Insert the thin slicing disc. Stand the scallions, tightly packed, in the feed tube and process.

Transfer the red pepper and scallion mixture to a 1-quart saucepan, cover with water and bring to a boil. Drain and squeeze between paper towels, removing as much moisture as possible. Set aside in a mixing bowl. (You should have about 1 cup.)

Preheat the oven to 250°F.; oil a 4½-cup ring mold.

Cut the reserved ½-inch square of red pepper into thin slices. Arrange the slices, scallion greens and carrot slices (if used) in the bottom of the prepared mold, making a decorative pattern (fig. 1).

Use ½ of the mousseline to line the inside of the mold with a ½-inch layer (fig. 2), smoothing to eliminate air bubbles.

Gently fold ½ of the remaining mousseline into the reserved cooked vegetables; spoon the mixture into the lined mold, smoothing the top of the vegetables (fig. 3).

Put the remaining mousseline into a pastry bag fitted with a ½-inch plain tip. Pipe the mousseline over the vegetable mixture to cover (fig. 4). Smooth the top. Tap the mold on a counter several times to release air bubbles. Place the mold on a baking sheet and bake in the center of the preheated oven for about 70 minutes or until the internal temperature reaches 155°F.

Meanwhile, 15 minutes before removing the terrine from the oven prepare the White Wine Sauce.

Remove the mold to a wire rack to cool for 10 to 15 minutes. Line a serving platter with a double thickness of paper towels. Place the platter and paper towels over the mold and invert. Do not remove the mold. Let stand for 5 minutes to drain. Carefully invert, removing the platter and paper towels. Run a knife around both edges of the mold. Wipe off the serving platter, place over the mold and invert again.

To serve, spoon some of the White Wine Sauce onto a plate and arrange two slices of the terrine on it, or serve the sauce separately.

Serves 12 to 16.

White Wine Sauce

4 tablespoons (½ stick) unsalted butter
2 large shallots, peeled and minced
1½ cups bottled clam broth or fish stock
1½ cups dry white wine
1 teaspoon sugar
4 teaspoons arrowroot or cornstarch
1 cup heavy cream
⅛ teaspoon freshly ground white pepper
⅛ teaspoon freshly grated nutmeg
  Salt

Heat the butter in a 1½-quart saucepan over moderate heat. Stir in the minced shallots and cook for 1 minute. Add the clam broth or fish stock, wine and sugar and bring to a boil over high heat. Continue cooking until the liquid is reduced to 2 cups, about 10 minutes. Strain through a sieve into a 4-cup measure.

Rinse out the saucepan. Return 1½ cups of the stock to the saucepan and set aside over low heat.

Stir the arrowroot into the remaining ½ cup of stock until dissolved; whisk the mixture into the reserved stock. Cook, stirring occasionally, until the sauce thickens, 3 to 5 minutes. Stir in the heavy cream, pepper, nutmeg and salt to taste and heat through.

Makes about 2 cups.

1. Making pattern in mold. 2. Lining mold with mousseline. 3. Smoothing vegetable mixture. 4. Piping mousseline over vegetable filling.

by Anne Lindsay Greer

Pasta is not often associated with Mexican-American food, yet it appears in many dishes in both Mexico and the bordering American states. I have always been disappointed with the blandness of most flavored pasta, so I set to work to develop my own recipes, with chili powder and fresh jalapeño chilies. The results are a red fettuccine, *picante* but not too stinging; and a sprightly green fettuccine, tasting distinctly of jalapeño peppers.

The following recipes use these Southwestern pastas in two salads and in two hot dishes. I feel that the red and green pastas will lead to many more variations and combinations, and I hope that you will feel free to experiment on your own.

The proportions given are for pasta that is made by hand. If you own a pasta-extruding machine, be sure to follow manufacturer's instructions concerning ingredient proportions.

SOUTHWESTERN PASTA
COOL & HOT

ROASTED PEPPERS AND SHRIMP SALAD WITH JALAPENO FETTUCCINE

      1 pound Jalapeño Fettuccine (recipe follows)
    ¼ cup loosely packed parsley leaves
      1 large garlic clove, peeled
    ¾ cup vegetable oil
    ⅓ cup white wine vinegar
      1 teaspoon salt
    ½ teaspoon dry mustard
    ¼ teaspoon freshly ground white pepper
        Pinch of sugar
      3 medium sweet red peppers
      3 fresh poblano chilies (see NOTE, follows); or 1 can (4–ounce) green chilies, drained, stemmed, seeded and cut into 2- by ¼-inch strips
      1 pound medium raw shrimp, unshelled
      3 medium zucchini (about 1 pound), trimmed and cut into lengths to fit feed tube vertically
    ½ cup (about 3 ounces) pignolias (pine nuts)
      8 ounces imported Queso Fresco cheese or feta cheese

Bring 4 quarts of salted water to a boil. Add the fettuccine and cook just until tender, 45 to 60 seconds. Do not overcook. Drain and set aside in a large serving dish or salad bowl.

Use the metal blade of a food processor and, with the machine running, drop the parsley and garlic through the feed tube and process until minced. Add the oil, vinegar, salt, mustard, pepper and sugar and pulse 3 or 4 times to mix. Pour ½ of the dressing over the fettuccine and toss well; set the remaining dressing aside in a small bowl.

Roast the red peppers on all sides under the broiler or, with a long fork or tongs, hold each one over a gas flame; cook, turning, until the skin is evenly blistered and blackened. Put the peppers in a plastic bag and place in the freezer for 10 minutes. Remove, peel off the skins, split open and remove the stems, seeds and veins. Cut the peppers into 2- by ¼-inch strips. Pat dry on paper towels and add to the fettuccine.

Repeat for the fresh chilies, but do not remove the veins.

Bring 1 quart of water to a boil. Add the shrimp, reduce the heat and simmer until just cooked through, 3 to 4 minutes. Drain and rinse under cold running water. Peel and devein the shrimp. Cut them in half lengthwise and add to the fettuccine.

Use the shredding disc to process the zucchini. Pat dry on paper towels and add to the fettuccine.

Heat 2 tablespoons of the reserved dressing in a small skillet over moderate heat. Add the pignolias and cook, stirring, until they are golden brown, 2 to 3 minutes. With a slotted spoon set aside to drain on paper towels.

Pour the remaining dressing over the salad, crumble the cheese on top and sprinkle with the reserved pignolias; toss well.

Makes 4 to 6 servings.

NOTE: When handling chili peppers wear rubber gloves: the oils in chilies may cause skin irritation.

Jalapeño Fettuccine

    ¼ cup loosely packed fresh cilantro leaves
      8 fresh jalapeño chilies or 12 fresh serrano chilies, halved, stemmed and seeded (see NOTE, above)
      3 large eggs
    2½ cups unbleached all-purpose flour
      1 tablespoon vegetable oil
    1½ teaspoons salt
        Cornmeal

Use the metal blade of a food processor to chop the cilantro, pulsing 6 to 8 times. With the machine running, drop the chilies through the feed tube and process for 10 seconds; add 1 of the eggs and continue processing until the chilies are minced, about 15 seconds. Add the remaining eggs, the flour, oil and salt and process until the dough forms a ball. (If the dough is too sticky to form a ball, add flour by tablespoons with the machine running. If it is too dry, add water by teaspoons.) Continue processing for 60 seconds more to knead the dough. Remove the dough, wrap in plastic wrap and let stand, at room temperature, for at least 30 minutes.

Sprinkle cornmeal over 2 cookie sheets; set aside.

Divide the dough into 6 portions. Shape 1 of the portions, keeping the rest covered, into a 4–inch cylinder. On a lightly floured surface roll out the dough into a long rectangle; the dough should be about ¹⁄₁₆-inch thick. Using a straight–edge as a guide, with a sharp knife cut the pasta lengthwise at ¼-inch intervals. Transfer to a reserved cookie sheet and toss to coat with cornmeal. Repeat for the remaining portions of dough, dividing the pasta between the cookie sheets.

The pasta will keep, refrigerated, for 2 to 3 days in a plastic bag; or frozen for up to 3 months.

Makes 1¼ pounds.

RED CHILI PASTA SALAD

All of the preparation may be done a day ahead, except for cutting up the avocado. Assemble the salad just before serving.

- ½ pound Red Chili Fettuccine (recipe follows)
- 1 large garlic clove, peeled
- ⅔ cup vegetable oil
- ⅓ cup white wine vinegar
- 2 tablespoons fresh lime juice
- 2 teaspoons salt
- ½ teaspoon dry mustard
- ¼ teaspoon freshly ground white pepper
  Pinch of paprika
- 4 fresh jalapeño chilies or 6 fresh serrano chilies (see NOTE, page 10)
- 6 corn tortillas
  Vegetable oil for deep frying
- 1 large whole skinless, boneless chicken breast (about 10 ounces)
- 8 ounces Monterey Jack cheese, chilled
- 1 medium onion, peeled and quartered
- 1 avocado

Bring 2 quarts of salted water to a boil. Add the Red Chili Pasta and cook just until tender, 45 to 60 seconds. Do not overcook. Drain and transfer to a large serving dish or salad bowl.

Use the metal blade of a food processor and, with the machine running, drop the garlic through the feed tube and process until minced. Add the oil, vinegar, lime juice, 1 teaspoon of the salt, mustard, pepper and paprika and pulse 3 or 4 times to mix. Pour ½ of the dressing over the pasta salad and toss well; set the remaining dressing aside in a small bowl.

Roast the chilies on all sides under the broiler or, with a long fork or tongs, hold each one over a gas flame; cook, turning, until the skin is evenly blistered and blackened. Put the chilies in a plastic bag and place in the freezer for 10 minutes. Remove, peel off the skins, split open and remove the stems and seeds. Cut the chilies into 2- by ¼-inch slices. Pat dry with paper towels and add to the pasta.

Cut the tortillas into ¼-inch strips and then diagonally at ⅓-inch intervals. Heat 2 inches of vegetable oil for deep frying in a 1½-quart saucepan to 375°F. Fry the tortillas, in several batches, stirring, until golden and crisp, about 35 seconds. Remove to paper towels to drain; sprinkle with remaining salt. Set aside.

Bring 1 quart of water to a simmer. Poach the chicken for 8 to 10 minutes or until done. Drain and let cool. Shred the chicken by hand and add

Red Chili Pasta Salad, top, and Roasted Peppers and Shrimp Salad with Jalapeño Fettuccine.

to the pasta.

Use the shredding disc to process the cheese. Add to the salad. Use the metal blade to chop the onion coarsely, pulsing 6 to 8 times. Add to the salad.

Peel and seed the avocado. Cut into ½-inch pieces and add to the salad. Pour the reserved dressing over the salad. Add the reserved tortillas and toss well. Serve immediately.

Makes 6 to 8 servings.

Red Chili Fettuccine

      3 tablespoons commercial chili powder (see NOTE, follows)
      2 cups unbleached all-purpose flour
   1½ teaspoons salt
      3 large eggs
      2 tablespoons water
   1½ teaspoons vegetable oil
         Cornmeal

Preheat the oven to 250°F. Sprinkle the chili powder over a cookie sheet and place it in the preheated oven for 8 to 10 minutes to toast the powder. Do not let it burn.

Use the metal blade of a food processor to mix the chili powder, flour and salt, pulsing 3 or 4 times. With the machine running, add the eggs, water and oil through the feed tube and process until the dough forms a ball. (If the dough is too sticky to form a ball, add flour by tablespoons with the machine running. If it is too dry add water by teaspoons.) Continue processing for 60 seconds to knead the dough. Remove, wrap in plastic wrap and let stand, at room temperature, for at least 30 minutes.

Sprinkle cornmeal over 2 cookie sheets; set aside.

Divide the dough into 6 equal portions. Shape 1 of the portions, keeping the rest covered, into a 4-inch cylinder. On a lightly floured surface roll out the cylinder into a long rectangle; the dough should be about ⅟₁₆-inch thick. Using a straight edge as a guide, with a sharp knife cut the dough lengthwise at ¼-inch intervals. Transfer the cut pasta to a reserved cookie sheet and toss to coat with cornmeal. Repeat for the remaining portions of dough, dividing the pasta between the cookie sheets.

The pasta will keep, refrigerated, for 2 to 3 days in a plastic bag; or frozen for up to 3 months.

Makes 1 pound.
NOTE: If the chili powder does not include additional spices, add 1 teaspoon ground cumin and 1 teaspoon garlic powder.

JALAPENO FETTUCCINE WITH MEXICAN CREAM

      2 medium sweet red peppers
      2 ounces (⅓ cup in ½-inch cubes) imported Parmesan cheese, at room temperature
   ½ cup loosely packed fresh cilantro leaves
      1 medium zucchini, trimmed and cut into lengths to fit feed tube vertically
   ½ pound Jalapeño Fettuccine (recipe on page 10)
      2 tablespoons unsalted butter
   ¾ cup Mexican Cream (recipe follows)

Roast the red peppers on all sides under the broiler or, with a long fork or tongs, hold each one over a gas flame; cook, turning, until the skin is evenly blistered and blackened. Put the peppers in a plastic bag and place in the freezer for 10 minutes. Remove, peel off the skins, split open and remove the stems, seeds and veins. Cut the peppers into 2- by ¼-inch slices. Set aside to drain on paper towels.

Use the metal blade of a food processor and, with the machine running, drop the cheese through the feed tube and process until finely chopped, about 1 minute. Set aside. Use the metal blade to chop the cilantro, pulsing 6 to 8 times or until coarsely chopped. Set aside.

Use the shredding disc to process the zucchini; set aside to drain on paper towels.

Bring 2 quarts of salted water to a boil. Add the fettuccine and cook just until tender, 45 to 60 seconds. Do not overcook. Drain and set aside.

Heat the butter in a large skillet over moderate heat. Stir in the reserved peppers and cook for 1 minute. Add the reserved cilantro and fettuccine and the Mexican Cream; toss to coat the pasta. Cook, stirring, just until the pasta is heated through. Remove the pan from the heat and stir in the reserved zucchini.

Transfer to a serving dish and sprinkle with the reserved Parmesan.

Makes 4 servings.

Mexican Cream

   ½ cup heavy cream
   ½ cup sour cream
      1 teaspoon fresh lime juice

In a small bowl combine all of the ingredients. Cover with plastic wrap and refrigerate for at least 2 hours before using. The mixture will keep for up to 1 week.

Makes 1 cup.

RED CHILI PASTA WITH CHORIZO

The inspiration for this recipe is one of my favorite dishes, Sopa de Fideo.

1 fresh green poblano chili (see NOTE, page 10); or 1 large green pepper

3 ounces (½ cup in ½-inch cubes) imported Parmesan cheese, at room temperature

1 large garlic clove, peeled

1 cup loosely packed fresh basil leaves

6 medium scallions, trimmed and cut to fit feed tube vertically

3 medium tomatoes, seeded

½ pound fresh chorizo, casings removed; or ½ pound bulk pork sausage mixed with 1 teaspoon chili powder

¾ cup beef broth

½ pound Red Chili Fettuccine (recipe on page 12)

Salt and freshly ground black pepper

Roast the chili or green pepper on all sides under the broiler or, with a long fork or tongs, hold it over a gas flame; cook, turning, until the skin is evenly blistered and blackened. Put it in a plastic bag and place in the freezer for 10 minutes. Remove, peel off the skin, split open and remove the stem and seeds. Pat dry with paper towels. Cut the chili into ½-inch pieces; set aside.

Use the metal blade of a food processor, and with the machine running, drop the cheese through the feed tube and process until finely chopped, about 1 minute. Set aside. With the machine running, drop the garlic through the feed tube and process until minced. Set aside. Use the metal blade to chop the basil, pulsing 8 to 10 times. Set aside. Insert the thin slicing disc and process the scallions. Set aside. Insert the French fry disc and process the tomatoes. Set aside, reserving ¼ cup for garnish.

Cook the chorizo in a medium skillet over moderate heat, about 5 minutes, breaking it up with a fork. Add the reserved chili pieces, garlic and scallions and cook, stirring, for 1 minute. Pour in the broth and reduce the heat to low. Continue cooking, covered, for 5 minutes, stirring occasionally.

Meanwhile, bring 2 quarts of salted water to a boil. Add the fettuccine and cook for 45 to 60 seconds or until just tender. Do not overcook. Drain well. Return to the pot and toss with the sausage mixture, reserved basil and tomatoes. Season with salt and pepper to taste. Transfer to a serving dish and garnish with the reserved ¼ cup tomatoes. Pass the reserved Parmesan.

Makes 4 to 6 servings.

Jalapeño Fettuccine with Mexican Cream, top, and Red Chili Pasta with Chorizo.

Home Wedding Buffet

by Abby Mandel

Last summer I had the happy experience of being married in my own home. Even though I chose to have the cooking done by others, it was important to me that the menu convey my feelings about food. My goal was to plan with a caterer a refreshing summer buffet menu for fifty guests. I wanted food that had unfettered flavors and expressed the spirit of the occasion. It took only one conversation with Ann Bloomstrand of Spice 'N Easy of Glen Ellyn, Illinois, to convince me that I'd found my catering group. Their penchant for good food, simply prepared, was similar to my own.

I was delighted with the results—a beautiful assemblage of seasonal foods. Because the menu was simple, it could easily become one for your own summertime celebrations. Even though the caterers are professionals, no dish they chose was so difficult that it could not be made by a home cook. By planning ahead and using the timetable on page 17, you—along with some help from your good neighbors and friends—should be able to prepare the buffet with ease.

(Spice 'N Easy is the name of both a shop and catering business run by Ann Bloomstrand, Lee Chalfant and Glenn Prange—three young people with fine cooking backgrounds.)

A Joyous Buffet. Inset: the hors d'oeuvres—clockwise from bottom—Shrimp Wrapped in Snow Peas, Red Potato Shells, and Cheese Straws. On the buffet table —clockwise from bottom —Tomato Cheese Tart, Garden Lettuce Salad, Boneless Leg of Lamb, Fresh Fruit Platter and Crudité with Spinach Herb Dipping Sauce.

SHRIMP WRAPPED IN SNOW PEAS

The shrimp and snow peas may be assembled up to 8 hours in advance; cover and refrigerate.

- ¼ cup loosely packed parsley leaves
- 1½ cups olive oil
- ¼ cup sherry vinegar
- 1 tablespoon fresh lemon juice
- 1 tablespoon Dijon mustard
- 2 teaspoons salt
- 1 teaspoon crushed dried rosemary
- ½ teaspoon sugar
  Freshly ground black pepper
- ⅓ cup vegetable oil
- 50 medium shrimp (about 2½ pounds), peeled and deveined
- 50 snow peas (about 1 pound), strings removed

Use the metal blade of a food processor to mince the parsley, processing for 10 seconds. Add the olive oil, vinegar, lemon juice, mustard, salt, rosemary, sugar and pepper to taste and process for 5 seconds to mix. Transfer the marinade to a 4-quart bowl and set aside.

Heat 2 tablespoons of the vegetable oil in a medium skillet over moderate heat. Cook 10 of the shrimp just until pink, about 2 minutes, turning once. Set aside. Repeat for the remaining shrimp, adding oil as necessary.

When the shrimp are cool enough to handle, but still warm, cut in half lengthwise. Add to the marinade and toss to coat the shrimp. Cover and refrigerate for at least 6 hours or overnight.

Bring 2 quarts of salted water to a boil. Add the snow peas and blanch for 30 seconds. Drain and run under cold running water to cool completely. Drain again and pat dry. Split the snow peas in half lengthwise. Wrap a snow pea half around a shrimp half and secure with a toothpick. Refrigerate until ready to serve.

Makes 100.

RED POTATO SHELLS WITH CREME FRAICHE AND CAVIAR

- 50 small waxy red new potatoes (about 6 pounds)
- 2 quarts vegetable oil
- 4 large baking potatoes (about 3 pounds), peeled and quartered
- 2½ cups Crème Fraîche (recipe follows)
- ½ cup loosely packed snipped fresh chives
- 2 teaspoons salt
- ½ teaspoon freshly ground white pepper
- 4½ ounces golden caviar (see NOTE, follows)
  Fresh dill, for garnish

Preheat the oven to 350°F. Put the new potatoes on a rack on a baking sheet and bake in the preheated oven just until tender and the potatoes are easily pierced with a knife, 25 to 30 minutes. Do not overcook.

When cool enough to handle cut the potatoes in half and then cut a thin slice off the ends. With a melon baller or small spoon, scoop out as much of the pulp as possible. Reserve the pulp for another use.

Heat the oil in a 3-quart saucepan to 350°F. Fry the potato shells, in several batches and without crowding, until they are lightly browned, about 3½ minutes, stirring. With a slotted spoon transfer to paper towels to drain upside down.

Meanwhile, bring 2 quarts of salted water to a boil. Add the baking potatoes and cook until very tender, about 15 minutes. Drain and transfer to a 3-quart mixing bowl. Mash the potatoes and let cool to room temperature. Add the Crème Fraîche, chives, salt and pepper. Use an electric hand beater, set on low, to beat the mixture until it is light and fluffy, about 2 minutes.

Transfer to a pastry bag fitted with a star tip. Fill the potato shells, mounding the mixture slightly. Spoon about ¼ teaspoon of caviar onto the top and garnish with a small sprig of fresh dill.

Makes 100.

NOTE: Golden caviar is an American product, the roe of whitefish from the Great Lakes. It is much less expensive than sturgeon caviar, and it freezes well. It is available at good fish markets or gourmet stores.

Crème Fraîche

- 1 cup sour cream
- 2 cups heavy cream
- 2 teaspoons fresh lemon juice

Put the sour cream in a large mixing bowl. Gradually whisk in the heavy cream until thoroughly blended. Cover with plastic wrap and put in a warm place for 8 to 24 hours or longer, until the mixture has thickened.

Place a plastic coffee filter holder or strainer over a mixing bowl and insert a filter paper. Pour the thickened cream into the filter. Cover with plastic wrap, refrigerate and leave to drain for 24 to 36 hours. Tear away the filter paper along its seam, transfer the Crème Fraîche to a bowl and stir in the lemon juice. Cover and refrigerate for up to 1 week.

Makes about 2½ cups.

CHEESE STRAWS

- ¾ pound imported Parmesan cheese, at room temperature, cut into 1-inch cubes
- 3 recipes Semi-Puff Pastry (recipe follows)
- 2 large egg whites, lightly beaten

Use the metal blade of a food processor and, with the machine running, drop ⅓ of the cheese through the feed tube and process until finely chopped, about 60 seconds. Set aside. Repeat for the remaining cheese.

On a lightly floured surface roll out 1 recipe of the Semi-Puff Pastry into a 20- by 12-inch rectangle; trim the edges. Brush the dough with ⅓ of the beaten egg whites and sprinkle the entire surface with ⅓ of the grated cheese (about 1 cup). Press the cheese into the dough with a rolling pin or with your hands.

With a sharp knife cut the dough crosswise at ½-inch intervals. Twist each strip 8 times. Put the strips on a buttered baking sheet and place in the freezer for 15 minutes or until firm.

Meanwhile, preheat the oven to 350°F.

Bake the cheese straws in the center of the preheated oven until lightly browned, 14 to 16 minutes. Transfer to a wire rack to cool completely.

Repeat for the remaining 2 recipes of puff pastry, the cheese and egg whites. The cheese straws may be kept in an airtight container for up to 24 hours.

Makes 120.

Semi-Puff Pastry

You will need to make 3 recipes or about 3¾ pounds for the Cheese Straws.

1 cup unbleached all-purpose flour (5 ounces), chilled in the freezer for at least 4 hours

¾ cup cake flour (3 ounces), chilled in the freezer for at least 4 hours

½ pound (2 sticks) unsalted butter, well chilled, cut into 16 pieces

⅛ teaspoon salt

½ cup plus 1 tablespoon ice water

With the metal blade in place, put the flours, butter and salt in the processor bowl. Process with 6 short pulses.

Remove the pusher from the feed tube of your processor. Turn on the machine and immediately add the ice water as fast as possible, about 2 seconds. Pulse until the ingredients just clump together, usually 5 short pulses. Transfer the contents to a floured surface. With a floured rolling pin, roll into a rectangle about 6 by 8 inches. Fold the dough in thirds. Rotate the dough so that a short edge is toward you.

Roll the dough into a rectangle about 12 by 6 inches and ½ inch thick. Fold the short edges to meet in the center and fold in half along the line where the edges

Preparation Timetable

RECIPES	UP TO 1 MONTH	UP TO 1 WEEK	UP TO 2 DAYS	UP TO 1 DAY	DAY OF THE WEDDING
Cheese Straws	Make Puff Pastry, freeze.	Shape cheese straws and freeze unbaked.		Bake cheese straws and keep in airtight container.	Arrange cheese straws.
Shrimp Wrapped in Snow Peas				Sauté shrimp and marinate. Blanch snow peas, split in half, refrigerate.	Assemble shrimp and snow peas.
Red Potato Shells with Crème Fraîche and Caviar		Make Crème Fraîche, refrigerate.	Bake and hollow out red potatoes, refrigerate.		Deep fry and assemble potato shells.
Crudités with Spinach Herb Dipping Sauce		Make Crème Fraîche and Mayonnaise, refrigerate.	Make Spinach Herb Dipping Sauce, refrigerate.	Prepare vegetables, wrap each ingredient separately, refrigerate.	Arrange crudité platter.
Tomato Cheese Tarts	Make pastry. Line pans with pastry and freeze unbaked.			Slice tomatoes and marinate; prebake Tart Shells.	Assemble and bake tarts. Assemble salad. Roast lamb.
Garden Lettuce Salad with Goat's Milk Cheese and Pignolias		Toast pignolias, refrigerate.	Make Vinaigrette, refrigerate.	Blanch green beans, refrigerate; wash and tear lettuce, refrigerate.	
Boneless Legs of Lamb with Peppercorn Mustard Crust			Marinate lamb.	Sear lamb on grill or under broiler, roll and tie, refrigerate.	
Fresh Fruit Platter				Prepare fruits, wrap each ingredient separately, refrigerate.	Arrange fruit platter.
Chocolate Truffles	Make and freeze.				Arrange truffles.
Three-Tier Wedding Cake	Make Génoise layers, freeze.	Make Soaking Syrup, refrigerate.		Make Buttercream; assemble Génoise layers separately, without final frosting.	Finish wedding cake.

meet. This is one double turn.

Rotate the dough so that a short edge is toward you and make a second double turn.

Wrap the dough in plastic wrap and refrigerate for 30 minutes before rotating and making final double turn.

Refrigerate the dough, wrapped, for at least 2 hours before using; or freeze for up to 1 month.

Makes about 1¼ pounds; enough for 40 cheese straws.

TOMATO CHEESE TARTS

The following ingredients make 1 tart; you will need to make 2 recipes. The tarts may be prepared up to 4 hours in advance and kept at room temperature. To reheat, put the pans into a cold oven, turn the oven to 350°F. and bake for 15 minutes or until heated through.

- 18- by 12-inch partially baked Tart Shell (recipe follows)
- ½ cup loosely packed parsley leaves
- 3 large garlic cloves, peeled
- 1 cup olive oil or vegetable oil
- 2 teaspoons dried basil
- 2 teaspoons salt
- 1 teaspoon dried oregano leaves
- 1 teaspoon dried thyme leaves
- ⅛ teaspoon sugar
  Freshly ground black pepper
- 16 small Italian plum tomatoes or 6 medium tomatoes (about 2 pounds), cored, ends cut flat
- 1 pound imported Emmenthal or Swiss cheese, at room temperature
- ¼ cup Dijon mustard

Use the metal blade of a food processor to mince the parsley, processing for 10 seconds. With the machine running, drop the garlic through the feed tube and process until minced. Add the oil, basil, salt, oregano, thyme, sugar and pepper to taste and process for 3 seconds. Carefully remove the metal blade and insert the medium slicing disc. Place the tomatoes cut side down in the feed tube and process using light pressure. Transfer the tomatoes and marinade to a 1-gallon plastic bag and seal with a wire twist. Place in another plastic bag, seal with a wire twist and refrigerate for at least 6 hours or overnight, turning the bag once or twice.

Preheat the oven to 350°F.

Use the shredding disc to process the cheese, using light pressure. Spread the mustard evenly over the Tart Shell and distribute the cheese over the tart. Arrange the tomatoes down the length of the tart in overlapping rows.

Bake the tart in the center of the preheated oven for 25 to 30 minutes. Remove to a wire rack and let stand for at least 10 minutes; cut the tart into 2-inch squares.

Makes 1 tart; fifty-four 2-inch squares.

Tart Shell
You will need to make 2 recipes for the Tomato Cheese Tarts.

- 2¼ cups unbleached all-purpose flour (11¼ ounces)
- 12 tablespoons (1½ sticks) unsalted butter (6 ounces), chilled and cut into 12 pieces
- ¾ teaspoon salt
- 1 large egg yolk
- 6 tablespoons ice water

Use the metal blade of a food processor to process the flour, butter and salt for 20 seconds or until the mixture resembles coarse meal. With the machine running pour the egg yolk and water through the feed tube and process just until the dough begins to come together. (If the dough does not come together, add water by teaspoons until it does.) Form the dough into a ball. Flatten it into a disc on plastic wrap, wrap lightly and refrigerate for 30 minutes.

Preheat the oven to 400°F.

On a lightly floured surface roll the chilled dough into a 20- by 14-inch rectangle. Transfer to an 18- by 12-inch jelly roll pan, pressing the dough gently against the bottom and sides, taking care not to stretch the dough. Press the dough into a rim and remove the excess dough. Prick the bottom with a fork. (The tart shell may be frozen in the pan, well wrapped, for up to 1 month.) Line the shell with parchment paper or aluminum foil and fill with dried beans. Bake in the center of the preheated oven for 15 minutes. Remove the paper and beans and return to the oven for 5 to 8 minutes more or until the pastry is set but not browned. Remove the pan to a wire rack.

Makes one 18- by 12-inch tart shell.

GARDEN LETTUCE SALAD WITH GOAT'S MILK CHEESE AND PIGNOLIAS
Select the lettuce according to what is available at your market; use the following list as a guide.

- 4 cups (about 20 ounces) pignolias (pine nuts)
- 4 pounds green beans, trimmed
- 8 heads radicchio lettuce, washed, dried and torn into bite-size pieces
- 8 heads Boston lettuce, washed, dried and torn into bite-size pieces
- 4 heads Bibb lettuce, washed, dried and torn into bite-size pieces
- 1 head red leaf lettuce, washed, dried and torn into bite-size pieces
- 1 head romaine lettuce, washed, dried and torn into bite-size pieces
- 1½ pounds goat's milk cheese
  Vinaigrette (recipe follows)

Preheat the oven to 400°F. To toast the pignolias, spread them on a cookie sheet and place in the preheated oven for about 6 minutes or until lightly browned, shaking the pan several times. Set aside.

Bring 2 quarts of salted water to a boil. Add ½ of the green beans and cook just until the beans are tender but still crisp, 4 to 6 minutes. Drain and refresh under cold running water. Drain and set aside. Repeat for the remaining beans.

To serve, put the lettuce in salad bowls. Add the reserved green beans. Crumble ⅔ of the cheese over the salad. Pour the Vinaigrette over the salad and toss. Crumble the remaining cheese over the salad and add the reserved toasted pignolias.

Serves 50.

Vinaigrette

  ½ cup sherry vinegar
  4 large egg yolks
1¼ tablespoons salt
  2 teaspoons freshly ground black pepper
  4 cups olive oil or vegetable oil

Use the metal blade of a food processor to process the vinegar, egg yolks, salt, pepper and 2 cups of the oil for 5 seconds. Transfer to a 2-quart mixing bowl and whisk in the remaining oil.

BONELESS LEGS OF LAMB WITH PEPPERCORN MUSTARD CRUST

  5 butterflied legs of lamb (each about 5½ pounds)
    Marinade (recipe follows)
  ¼ cup black peppercorns
  ¼ cup green peppercorns
  ¼ cup white peppercorns
2½ cups Dijon mustard
  1 tablespoon dried basil
  2 teaspoons crushed dried rosemary
  1 teaspoon dried tarragon
  1 teaspoon sugar
    Rosemary sprigs, for garnish

Put each leg of lamb into a jumbo-size plastic bag. Evenly distribute the Marinade among the bags, seal with a wire twist and refrigerate for at least 8 hours or overnight, turning occasionally.

Preheat the broiler or prepare a fire on an outdoor grill. Remove the lamb from the marinade. Sear each leg, placing it 4 to 6 inches from the heat, for about 4 minutes a side or until the meat is browned.

When the meat is cool enough to handle, roll up each leg, starting with a narrow side, into a cylinder. Place seam side down and tie string around the lamb at 1-inch intervals to secure it; then tie it lengthwise.

Coarsely crush the black, green and white peppercorns in a mortar with a pestle, or with a

rolling pin. Stir together and set aside.

In a 1-quart mixing bowl stir together the mustard, basil, rosemary, tarragon and sugar. Spread ⅕ of the mixture evenly over each leg. Pat each leg with ⅕ (about 2 tablespoons) of the reserved crushed pepper.

Preheat the oven to 500°F.

Place a rack in a roasting pan and pour in 2 cups of water. Place 1 or 2, if possible, rolled legs on the rack (they should not be touching) and roast in the center of the preheated oven for 30 to 35 minutes for rare meat or until the internal temperature reaches 120°F.

Remove the lamb from the oven and let stand for at least 10 minutes or up to 1 hour before carving. Slice thinly and arrange on a serving platter. Garnish with rosemary sprigs. Serve warm or at room temperature.

Serves 50.

Marinade

  2 tablespoons black peppercorns
  2 tablespoons green peppercorns
  2 tablespoons white peppercorns
10 large garlic cloves, peeled and halved
  1 bottle (25-ounce) dry red wine
  ¾ cup olive oil or vegetable oil
  ¼ cup crushed dried rosemary
  1 tablespoon salt

Coarsely crush all the peppercorns in a mortar with a pestle, or with a rolling pin. Set aside.

Use the metal blade of a food processor and, with the machine running, drop the garlic through the feed tube and process until minced. Add ½ of the wine, the oil, rosemary, salt and reserved crushed pepper and process for 5 seconds. Transfer to a 2-quart mixing bowl and stir in the remaining wine.

Makes about 4 cups.

FRESH FRUIT PLATTER

Choose fruits according to what is available at your market. Use the following list as a guide. You may prepare the fruit a day in advance. Wrap each fruit separately and refrigerate.

3 cantaloupes, halved, seeded, cut into ¾ inch slices and rind removed
2 honeydew melons, halved, seeded, cut into ¾-inch slices and rind removed
6 papayas, peeled, halved, seeded and cut into 1-inch cubes
2 pineapples, peeled, halved, cut into ⅓-inch slices and cored
3 pints strawberries
  Lemon leaves, for garnish (optional)

Arrange the fruits on serving platters. Garnish with lemon leaves, if used.

Serves 50.

CRUDITES WITH SPINACH HERB DIPPING SAUCE

Select vegetables according to what is available at your market; use the following list as a guide. The vegetables may be prepared a day in advance. Wrap separately in plastic wrap and refrigerate.

  Eggplant
  Fresh lemon juice
  Spinach Herb Dipping Sauce (recipe follows)
3 pounds young asparagus, white part removed and tough stems peeled
1 pound green beans, trimmed
1 pound wax beans, trimmed
2 bunches broccoli, flowerets only, separated into bite-size pieces
2 bunches carrots, trimmed, peeled and cut into ⅓-inch diagonal slices
2 heads cauliflower, flowerets only, separated into bite-size pieces
1 pound endive, trimmed and leaves separated
3 pounds mushrooms, stems trimmed
2 pounds oyster mushrooms, stems trimmed, quartered
1 pound fresh peas, shelled
4 large green peppers, cored, seeded and cut into ½-inch strips
4 large red peppers, cored, seeded and cut into ½-inch strips
4 large yellow peppers, cored, seeded and cut into ½-inch strips
6 bunches scallions, trimmed
3 pints cherry tomatoes, stemmed
3 pounds zucchini, trimmed and cut into ⅓-inch diagonal slices
  Leafy greens, such as beet greens, Swiss chard or kale, for garnish (optional)

Use 1 or more eggplants to serve the Spinach Herb Dipping Sauce. Lay the eggplant on its side and cut off a 1-inch slice horizontally, leaving the stem. Hollow out the eggplant, leaving ¼-inch-thick skin. Rub the top edge and inside with lemon juice and fill with the sauce. Arrange the vegetables around the filled eggplant. Garnish with the greens, if used.
  Serves 50.

Spinach Herb Dipping Sauce

½ cup water
2 pounds fresh spinach, stems trimmed, washed
4 large scallions, trimmed, cut into 2-inch lengths
1 large bunch Italian flat leaf parsley, stemmed
1 bunch watercress, stemmed
1 bunch fresh dill, stemmed
¼ cup snipped chives
4 cups Mayonnaise (recipe follows)
2 cups Crème Fraîche (recipe on page 16)
1½ teaspoons salt
  Freshly ground white pepper

Bring the water to a boil in a 4-quart saucepan. Add the spinach, cover and cook over moderate heat just until wilted, 3 to 4 minutes, stirring occasionally. Drain and refresh under cold running water. Drain again; press the spinach dry in a towel. Set aside.

  Use the metal blade of a food processor to process the scallions, parsley, watercress, dill and chives, processing for 25 seconds or until they are minced. Add ½ of the reserved spinach and pulse 6 to 8 times to chop the spinach coarsely. Add 1 cup of the Mayonnaise and 1 cup of the Crème Fraîche and process for 10 seconds, stopping to scrape the bowl. Transfer to a 3-quart mixing bowl.

  Use the metal blade to chop the remaining spinach, pulsing 6 to 8 times. Add 1 cup of the mayonnaise and the remaining 1 cup of crème fraîche and process until mixed, scraping the bowl once. Add to the mixing bowl and stir in the remaining 2 cups of mayonnaise. Add the salt and pepper to taste and stir to mix.

  Cover and refrigerate until needed. The sauce will keep for up to 2 days. Adjust seasoning before serving.
  Makes about 8 cups.

Mayonnaise

3 large eggs
3 tablespoons fresh lemon juice
3 tablespoons Dijon mustard
¼ teaspoon salt
3¾ cups vegetable oil

Use the metal blade of a food processor to process the eggs, lemon juice, mustard, salt and 2 tablespoons of the oil for 60 seconds. With the machine running, slowly dribble the remaining oil through the feed tube. As the mayonnaise thickens the oil may be added more quickly. Adjust the seasoning. Cover tightly and store in the refrigerator for up to 1 week.
  Makes about 4½ cups.

THREE-TIER WEDDING CAKE

A lovely accompaniment to the cake is a large bowl of fresh raspberries, blueberries and blackberries, served with a pureed raspberry sauce.

2 recipes Génoise (recipe follows)
  Soaking Syrup (recipe follows)
4 recipes Vanilla Buttercream (recipe follows)
10 pints small strawberries, hulled
  Fresh flowers, for decoration

Cut out 4 heavy cardboard circles: 6½, 9½, 11½ and 15 inches in diameter. Set aside.

Cut four 3½- by ¼-inch wooden dowels; set aside.

Using a serrated knife, carefully remove the golden brown crust from the top of the 12-inch Génoise layer and discard. Level the layer as much as possible. Split the génoise in half horizontally (fig. 1). Brush cut side of each layer with about ¾ cup Soaking Syrup (fig. 2).

Spread a small amount of Vanilla Buttercream on the reserved 11½-inch cardboard circle. Center a 12-inch layer of génoise, syrup side up, on the cardboard circle, making sure no cardboard shows. Spread ⅓-inch of buttercream on top of the centered layer (fig. 3). Arrange strawberries on the buttercream, placing the hulled end into the icing (fig. 4). The strawberries should be nearly uniform in height. (If small strawberries are unavailable, slice large ones in half lengthwise and place cut side down.)

Fill a pastry bag fitted with a ½-inch plain tip with buttercream. Pipe the buttercream in the spaces between the strawberries (fig. 5). Carefully position the remaining génoise layer, syrup side down, on top of the strawberries (fig. 6). Pipe buttercream between the strawberries on the side of the layers (fig. 7); run a spatula around the side to smooth. Brush off any loose crumbs and spread a thin layer of buttercream on the top and side of the génoise (fig. 8). Refrigerate, uncovered, for 4 to 6 hours or overnight.

Repeat for the remaining génoise layers but use about ½ cup soaking syrup to brush each 10-inch layer and about ⅓ cup syrup for each 7-inch layer. Also

spread buttercream on the 9½- and 6½-inch cardboard circles and center corresponding 10-inch and 7-inch layers over them.

Reserve ½ cup of the remaining buttercream. With a long thin spatula spread the remaining buttercream evenly and smoothly over the top and side of the layers. Refrigerate the layers for 1 to 2 hours to set icing.

To assemble the cake, mark 4 evenly spaced dots about 3½ inches in from the edge of the 12-inch layer. To secure the bottom layer insert the reserved dowels at the dots, pushing them through to the cardboard. Wrap the reserved 15-inch cardboard circle with florist's foil. Carefully center the 12-inch layer on it; center the 10-inch layer on the 12-inch; and center the 7-inch layer on the 10-inch. Touch up with reserved buttercream. Refrigerate the cake until ready to serve.

Decorate with fresh flowers.

Serves 50.

Génoise

You will need to make 2 recipes of Génoise. One recipe is for a 7- by 3-inch round cake pan and a 10- by 2-inch cake pan; the other recipe is for a 12- by 2-inch cake pan.

- 1¼ cups plus 2 tablespoons (5¼ ounces) cake flour
- 1 cup plus 1 tablespoon (5¼ ounces) unbleached all-purpose flour
- 12 large eggs
- 1½ cups sugar
- 1 teaspoon pure vanilla extract
- 8 tablespoons (1 stick) unsalted butter, clarified and kept warm

1. Cutting the génoise in half horizontally.
2. Brushing with soaking syrup.
3. Spreading ⅓-inch layer of buttercream.
4. Arranging strawberries on buttercream.

5. Piping buttercream between strawberries.
6. Positioning génoise on strawberries.
7. Piping buttercream between layers.
8. Spreading thin layer of buttercream.

Three-Tier Wedding Cake and baskets filled with Chocolate Truffles.

Butter and flour a 7- by 3-inch round cake pan and a 10- by 2-inch cake pan; or a 12- by 2-inch cake pan. Set aside. Preheat the oven to 350°F.

Sift the flours together; sift again and set aside.

Fill a 4-quart saucepot ¼ full of warm water and place over moderately low heat. Put the eggs in an 8-quart stainless steel or copper mixing bowl and place on top of the saucepot, making certain the bottom of the mixing bowl does not touch the water. Using an electric hand mixer at medium speed, beat the eggs until frothy, about 1 minute. Continue beating while slowly adding the sugar, 2 tablespoons at a time, making certain the sugar is well blended before adding more. Continue beating for 10 minutes or until the eggs are thick and lightly colored. Remove the mixing bowl from the heat and beat at medium-high speed until the mixture has tripled in volume, about 15 minutes.

Sift ¼ cup of the reserved flour over the surface and gently fold it in with a large rubber spatula. Continue sifting and folding in the flour ¼ cup at a time. Stir the vanilla into the butter and fold gently into the batter. Be careful not to overfold.

Transfer the batter to the prepared pans (about 5 cups of batter for the 7- by 3-inch pan, and about 7 cups for the 10- by 2-inch pan) or pan and bake in the center of the preheated oven for 30 to 35 minutes or until a cake tester inserted in the center comes out clean and the cake just begins to pull away from the side of the pan.

Remove from the oven and immediately invert onto a wire rack to cool completely. Wrap the cakes airtight and refrigerate overnight. The cakes may also be frozen, well wrapped, for up to 1 month.

Makes 1 recipe, about 12 cups.

Soaking Syrup

1½ cups water
¾ cup sugar
1¾ cups Grand Marnier

In a 1-quart saucepan bring the water and sugar to a boil, stirring. Remove from the heat; let stand until it comes to room temperature. Stir in the Grand Marnier.

Makes about 3½ cups.

Vanilla Buttercream
You will need 4 recipes for the wedding cake.

2 cups granulated sugar
2 tablespoons light corn syrup
½ cup water
4 large egg whites
    Pinch of salt
10 tablespoons (1¼ sticks) unsalted butter, at room temperature

4 teaspoons pure vanilla extract

In a 2-quart saucepan, bring the sugar, corn syrup and water to a boil, stirring. Boil gently, without stirring, until the temperature reaches 240°F. on a candy thermometer. Set aside.

In a 4-quart mixing bowl, beat the egg whites and salt with an electric mixer at high speed until stiff peaks form. Add the reserved hot syrup slowly in a fine, steady stream. Continue beating for about 5 minutes more or until the mixture is very thick and has cooled to room temperature. Set aside.

In another large mixing bowl, without washing the beaters, beat the butter and vanilla until light and fluffy. Gradually beat in the reserved egg white mixture, a few tablespoons at a time.

The buttercream may be made a day ahead and refrigerated. To use, let stand, at room temperature, until the buttercream may easily be spread.

Makes 1 recipe, about 4 cups.

CHOCOLATE TRUFFLES

1½ cups heavy cream
8 tablespoons (1 stick) unsalted butter
1 pound plus 3 ounces semi-sweet chocolate, broken into pieces
6 tablespoons sugar
    Pinch of salt
¼ cup Cognac
½ cup unsweetened cocoa

Butter three 17- by 14-inch baking sheets. Set aside.

In a 1-quart saucepan bring the cream and butter to a simmer.

Meanwhile, use the metal blade of a food processor to chop the chocolate with the sugar and salt, pulsing 6 times and then processing until the chocolate is finely chopped. With the machine running, slowly pour the simmering cream mixture through the feed tube; continue processing until the chocolate has melted and the mixture is smooth, stopping twice to scrape the bowl. Add the Cognac and process 10 seconds.

Transfer the mixture to a 3-quart mixing bowl and place it in a pan of ice water. With a wooden spoon beat the mixture until it has thickened enough to hold its shape, 10 to 12 minutes. Spoon it into a pastry bag fitted with a ½-inch plain tip. Pipe 1-inch rounds onto the reserved baking sheets about ¾ inch apart. Place in the freezer until the rounds are frozen.

Put the cocoa into a plastic bag. Add 15 frozen truffles and shake to coat them. Remove, tap off excess cocoa and return to the freezer until needed. The truffles may be frozen, well wrapped, for up to 1 month.

Makes about 175.

*A Weighty Batch of Pound Cakes.
Counterclockwise from below: Cinna-
mon Walnut, Raisin-Ringed Rum,
Chocolate, Scotch, Plain, Cinnamon
Walnut and slices of Citrus.*

PROCESSOR EASE —POUND CAKE

Pound cake—so called because the original recipe called for a pound each of flour, butter, sugar and eggs—is a universal favorite. To modern tastes, however, the classic cake is somewhat dense and heavy. By changing the proportions of the main ingredients, we came up with Basic Light Pound Cake, perceptibly lighter than the classic version yet buttery and moist.

Basic Light Pound Cake and its variations are quickly and simply made. Formerly, the eggs were separated and the whites beaten and then incorporated into the batter; with the food processor

method these steps are eliminated.

Good as they are just out of the oven, these cakes are even better the second day. Toasted, with butter, they are delicious.

BASIC LIGHT POUND CAKE

To measure the cake flour, stir the flour, scoop it into the measure and sweep off the excess flour.

- 1⅓ cups cake flour
- ¾ teaspoon baking powder
- ¼ teaspoon salt
- ¾ cup sugar
- 11 tablespoons unsalted butter, cut into 11 pieces, at room temperature
- 4 large eggs
- 1½ teaspoons pure vanilla extract

Preheat the oven to 325°F. Butter and flour an 8½- by 4½- by 2½-inch loaf pan. Set aside.

Use the metal blade of a food processor to mix the flour, baking powder and salt, pulsing 6 to 8 times. Set aside.

Use the metal blade to process the sugar and butter, pulsing 3 times and then processing for 30 seconds or until smooth, stopping once to scrape down the bowl. With the machine running add the eggs, 1 at a time, through the feed tube and process for 60 seconds, scraping the bowl twice. Add the vanilla and process 10 seconds. Add the reserved flour mixture, pulse 4 times, scrape down the bowl and pulse 4 to 6 times or until well mixed.

Pour the batter into the prepared loaf pan and bake in the center of the preheated oven for 50 minutes or until a cake tester inserted into the center comes out clean.

Remove the pan to a wire rack and let cool for 10 minutes. Turn the cake out and let cool completely.

Makes 1 pound cake.

Walnut and Cinnamon Pound Cake

Add 1 cup walnut halves and ½ teaspoon ground cinnamon to the ingredient list and use 1 cup sugar.

Follow the directions for Basic Light Pound Cake but in a 1-quart saucepan cover the walnuts with water and bring to a boil. Drain and rinse under cold running water. Drain and pat dry with paper towels. Spread on a cookie sheet and bake in a preheated 350°F. oven until they just begin to color, 8 to 10 minutes. Cool completely. Use the metal blade to chop the toasted walnuts with the flour, baking powder, salt and cinnamon, pulsing 3 or 4 times and then processing 8 seconds or until the walnuts are coarsely chopped. Continue with the recipe.

Citrus Pound Cake

Add the rind of 1 small orange and 1 small lemon to the ingredient list, removing the rind with a vegetable peeler or sharp knife and cutting it into ¼-inch strips.

Follow the directions for Basic Light Pound Cake but use the metal blade of a food processor to chop the orange and lemon rind with the sugar before adding the butter, pulsing 3 or 4 times and then processing for 60 seconds or until finely chopped. Then add the butter and continue with the recipe.

Chocolate Pound Cake

Substitute ⅓ cup unsweetened cocoa for the same amount of cake flour to the ingredient list and use 1 tablespoon pure vanilla extract.

Follow the directions for Basic Light Pound Cake adding the cocoa with the flour, baking powder and salt.

Scotch Pound Cake

Add 2 tablespoons Scotch to the ingredient list and use only 1 teaspoon pure vanilla extract.

Follow the directions for Basic Light Pound Cake adding the Scotch with the vanilla.

Raisin-Ringed Rum Pound Cake

The chopped raisins decoratively "ring" the bottom and sides of the pound cake.

Add ½ cup golden raisins and ¼ cup dark rum to the ingredient list and use only 1 teaspoon pure vanilla extract.

Follow the directions for Basic Light Pound Cake but add the raisins with the flour, baking powder and salt, pulsing 3 or 4 times and processing for 1 minute or until the raisins are chopped to a medium coarseness. Continue with the recipe, adding the rum with the vanilla.

A Touch of Saffron

The world's most precious spice is saffron, the dried stigmas of Crocus sativus. Each blue flower

by Nika Hazelton

bears three small, deep orange-yellow threads which must be plucked out by hand. For one pound of usable saffron, from 70,000 to 225,000 flowers are used. The vast quantity of flowers and the amount of hand labor needed to handle them account for its astronomical price.

On the bright side, a little saffron goes a long way. It gives both zest and vividness to familiar foods, and it has since antiquity. Greeks and Romans prized it. It is thought that conquering Moors introduced it to Spain, where it still plays an important part in cooking.

Saffron crocuses also grow in the Middle East and in northern India. Strength may vary, but all true saffron imparts a golden yellow to food, perfumes it gently and imbues it with an inimitable flavor, which reminds me a little of bitter honey. It is unmistakable in any dish. The crushed threads must be steeped in some liquid before use, to release the essential oils and rich color.

Be wary: there is no such substance as cheap saffron. Bargains do not exist. What you get may be adulterated turmeric or even ground safflower or marigold petals, any of which will color food, but not perfume it. Saffron is sold both in threads and in ground form. Because of the danger of substitution, it is usually safest to buy the threads.

If you have difficulty pulverizing saffron threads by themselves, the staff of THE PLEASURES OF COOKING suggests trying this method using salt. Put 1 tablespoon salt and 1 tablespoon saffron threads in a mortar, preferably a stone or ceramic one. Start grinding the saffron and the salt, using the pestle in a circular motion with firm pressure (fig. 1). Keep grinding until the threads of saffron have completely disappeared (fig. 2). Use the amount specified in the recipe.

RISOTTO ALLA MILANESE WITH CHICKEN LIVER SAUCE

This is a classic saffron rice dish of northern Italy. With a salad this dish is perfect for lunch or supper. The risotto may also be made without the sauce; it is excellent with a roast. Unlike a pilaf, risotto is creamy yet chewy. The secret of making risotto is adding liquid to the rice only as the rice has absorbed the previous addition of liquid—and stirring all the time the rice is being prepared.

Chicken Liver Sauce

- ½ cup loosely packed parsley leaves
- 1 small onion, peeled and quartered
- ¼ pound pancetta or blanched lean bacon, chilled, cut into 1-inch pieces
- ½ pound mushrooms, cleaned and ends trimmed
- 3 tablespoons unsalted butter
- 1 pound chicken livers, trimmed
- ½ cup dry Marsala
- ¼ teaspoon ground sage
  Salt and freshly ground black pepper
  Beurre manié: 1 tablespoon unbleached all-purpose flour blended with 1 tablespoon unsalted butter

Risotto alla Milanese

- 4 to 5 cups chicken broth, heated
- ½ teaspoon pulverized saffron threads
- 3 ounces (½ cup in ½-inch cubes) imported Parmesan cheese, at room temperature
- 1 small onion, peeled and quartered
- 7 tablespoons unsalted butter
- ¼ cup chopped beef marrow (optional)
- 2 cups imported arborio rice
- ½ cup dry white wine
  Salt and freshly ground black pepper
- 1 tablespoon minced fresh parsley, for garnish

To make the Chicken Liver Sauce, use the metal blade of a food processor to mince the parsley, processing for 10 seconds. Set aside.

Use the metal blade to mince the onion, pulsing 6 to 8 times; set aside.

Use the metal blade to mince the pancetta, pulsing 6 to 8 times; set aside.

Use the thin slicing disc to process the mushrooms; set aside.

Heat 2 tablespoons of the butter in a medium skillet over moderately high heat. Cook the reserved mushrooms, in 2 batches, stirring, until browned, about 2 minutes. With a slotted spoon remove the mushrooms and set aside.

Add the remaining 1 tablespoon of butter and the pancetta to the skillet and cook, stirring, until the pancetta is lightly browned, 1 to 2 minutes. Remove and set aside.

Discard all but 2 tablespoons of the fat from the skillet and cook the chicken livers, in 2 batches, stirring, until browned but still pink in the center, 2 to 3 minutes. Do not overcook. With a slotted spoon transfer the livers to a cutting board and cut them into quarters. Set aside.

Add the reserved minced onion to the skillet and cook, stirring, until the onion is soft, 1 to 2 minutes. Stir in the parsley and pancetta; add the Marsala and sage and cook 1 minute more. Add salt and pepper to taste. Stir in the beurre manié by teaspoons until the sauce has thickened and has the consistency of heavy cream. Add the reserved livers and mushrooms, and set the pan aside while you make the risotto.

To make the Risotto alla Milanese, pour ½ cup of the hot broth in a 1-cup measure, stir in the saffron and set aside.

Use the metal blade and, with the machine running, drop the Parmesan through the feed tube and process until it is finely chopped, about 1 minute. Set aside.

Use the metal blade to mince the onion, pulsing 6 to 8 times; set aside.

In a 4-quart saucepan heat 4 tablespoons of the butter and the marrow, if used, over moderate heat. Add the reserved minced onion and cook, stirring, until it is soft but not browned, 1 to 2 minutes. Stir in the rice and cook until it turns translucent, 1 to 2 minutes. Reduce the heat to low, add the white wine and cook, stirring, until all the liquid has been absorbed, 3 to 5 minutes. Then add the reserved broth and saffron mixture and continue cooking, stirring constantly, until the broth has been absorbed. Repeat for the remaining broth, adding ½ cup at a time and making sure the broth has been absorbed before adding more liquid, until the rice is tender. This should take 35 to 40 minutes. Add salt and pepper to taste.

Remove the pan from the heat and stir in the remaining 3 tablespoons of butter and the reserved Parmesan cheese. Transfer to a heated serving dish. Keep warm while you finish the sauce.

Return the skillet with the liver and mushroom mixture to moderate heat and cook, stirring, just until the ingredients are heated through, about 1 minute.

Make a well in the center of the risotto, pour the sauce into the well and garnish the rice with the minced parsley. Serve immediately.

Makes 6 to 8 servings.

SCHWENKFELDER SAFFRON CAKE

This recipe was given to me at the Kutztown Fair, in Pennsylvania, by a member of the Schwenkfelder religious community, in 1964. It is a good, plain coffee cake, enriched by its crumb topping.

   1 small all-purpose potato, peeled and halved
   1 teaspoon dry yeast
  ½ cup sugar
  ¼ teaspoon pulverized saffron threads
 1⅓ tablespoons hot water
 3¼ cups unbleached all-purpose flour
   9 tablespoons unsalted butter, cut into 9 pieces
  ⅓ cup milk
   1 large egg
  ⅛ teaspoon salt
    Crumb Topping (recipe follows)

In a 1-quart saucepan cook the potato in salted boiling water until soft. Drain, reserving ⅓ cup of the water; let the potato water cool to warm (105° to 115°F.) and stir in the yeast. In a small mixing bowl mash the potato. Stir in 3 tablespoons of the sugar. Pour in the reserved yeast mixture and blend thoroughly. Cover with oiled plastic wrap and set aside in a warm place (75° to 80°F.) to rise for 3 hours.

Combine the saffron and hot water; set aside.

Use the metal blade of a food processor to process 1½ cups of the flour, 8 tablespoons of the butter, the remaining sugar, the milk, egg, salt and reserved saffron and reserved yeast mixtures, pulsing 3 or 4 times and then processing for 15 seconds or until thoroughly mixed, stopping to scrape down the bowl as necessary. Transfer the dough to an oiled 1½-quart mixing bowl, cover and set aside in a warm place to rise until light and spongy, about 1½ hours.

Put the remaining 1¾ cups of flour in the bowl of a food processor with the metal blade, add the risen dough and pulse 6 to 8 times or just until the flour is incorporated. The dough should be soft but not sticky. (If it is too sticky, add additional flour, 2 tablespoons at a time, and process for 5 seconds more.)

Remove the dough and shape it into a ball. Place in an oiled 2-quart mixing bowl, turning to coat the dough. Cover and set aside in a warm place to let rise until doubled in volume, 3 to 4 hours; or refrigerate overnight.

Punch down the dough and transfer it to a lightly floured surface. Roll out the dough to a ⅓-inch thickness, about 13 inches in diameter. Place on a greased and floured 17- by 14-inch cookie sheet, cover and set aside in a warm place to let rise until almost doubled in volume, about 1 hour. (If the dough has been refrigerated, the rising time will take about 2 hours.)

Clockwise from top: Risotto alla Milanese with Chicken Liver Sauce, Schwenkfelder Saffron Cake and Stuffed Baked Eggs with Poulette Sauce.

Preheat the oven to 325°F.

Melt the remaining tablespoon of butter and brush the top of the cake. Sprinkle evenly with the Crumb Topping and bake in the center of the preheated oven for 25 to 30 minutes or until lightly browned. Transfer to a wire rack and let cool completely.

Makes 10 to 12 servings.

Crumb Topping

⅔ cup unbleached all-purpose flour
⅔ cup firmly packed light brown sugar
5 tablespoons unsalted butter, cut into 5 pieces, chilled
⅓ teaspoon ground cinnamon

Use the metal blade of a food processor to mix all of the ingredients, pulsing 6 to 8 times or until the mixture resembles coarse meal.

STUFFED BAKED EGGS WITH POULETTE SAUCE

Fried toast points or boiled rice are an excellent accompaniment.

8 large eggs, hard cooked, shells removed
4 tablespoons (½ stick) unsalted butter plus butter for dish
1 tablespoon minced onion or shallot
¼ cup any combination minced fresh oregano, sage, tarragon and thyme; or 2 tablespoons any combination dried oregano, sage, tarragon and thyme
½ cup plus 2 tablespoons heavy cream
¼ teaspoon paprika
Salt and freshly ground white pepper
3 tablespoons unbleached all-purpose flour
1⅔ cups chicken broth
⅛ teaspoon pulverized saffron threads
1 teaspoon lemon juice
Parsley sprigs, for garnish

Butter a shallow 9-inch-round baking dish and set aside.

Cut the eggs in half lengthwise. To keep the eggs stationary while baking, cut off a thin slice from the rounded bottom of each white, discarding the thin slices. With a small spoon carefully remove the yolks to the bowl of a food processor. Set aside the whites. Use the metal blade to process the egg yolks until smooth, 35 to 45 seconds.

Heat 1 tablespoon of the butter in a small skillet over moderate heat. Add the onion and cook, stirring, until soft but not browned, about 2 minutes. Stir in the herbs and cook 30 seconds more.

Add the onion-herb mixture, 2 tablespoons of the heavy cream, the paprika and salt and pepper to taste to the egg yolks, pulse 3 or 4 times and then process for 10 seconds or until smooth, stopping once to scrape the bowl.

Fill the reserved egg whites with the egg yolk mixture, mounding it and smoothing the top into a dome. Place the eggs in the prepared baking dish and set aside while you make the sauce.

Preheat the oven to 400°F.

Heat the remaining 3 tablespoons of butter in a 1½-quart saucepan over moderate heat. Whisk in the flour and cook for about 1 minute; do not let the flour brown. Add the chicken broth and saffron, reduce the heat to moderately low and cook, whisking constantly, until the sauce is smooth and has thickened, 5 to 8 minutes. Whisk in the remaining cream and continue cooking until the sauce is heated through.

Remove the pan from the heat and whisk in the lemon juice; season to taste. Spoon some of the sauce over each of the stuffed eggs; pour the remaining sauce around the eggs into the baking dish.

Place the baking dish in the center of the preheated oven and bake 5 to 7 minutes or until the eggs are heated through. Garnish with parsley sprigs and serve immediately.

Makes 4 servings.

ICED CHICKEN AND SAFFRON SOUP

2 tablespoons unsalted butter
2 medium Granny Smith or McIntosh apples (about 12 ounces), peeled, quartered, cored and sliced
1 medium onion, peeled and thinly sliced
3 cups chicken broth
1 cup dry white wine
½ teaspoon pulverized saffron threads
Salt and freshly ground white pepper
½ boneless, skinless chicken breast (about 4 ounces)
1 cup light cream
1 tablespoon minced parsley
1 tablespoon minced sweet red pepper

Heat the butter in a 2-quart saucepan over low heat. Add the apple and onion slices and cook, stirring often, until they are soft but not browned, about 20 minutes.

Stir in the chicken broth, wine and saffron, and bring to a boil over high heat; reduce the heat to low and simmer, covered, for 10 minutes, stirring often.

Strain the broth through a fine sieve into a 3-quart

mixing bowl. Use the metal blade of a food processor to puree the apple-onion solids, processing for about 30 seconds and stopping once to scrape down the bowl. Strain the puree through the sieve into the broth. Add salt and pepper to taste. Refrigerate for at least 2 hours or overnight, covering with plastic wrap after 2 hours.

Meanwhile, bring 1 quart of water to a simmer. Poach the chicken for 8 to 10 minutes or until done. Remove the chicken and let cool for 15 minutes. Cover and refrigerate.

When ready to serve, cut the reserved chicken breast into ¼-inch pieces. Stir the chicken and the cream into the soup. Transfer to a tureen and sprinkle with the parsley and red pepper.

Makes about 6 cups.

CHICKEN IN SAFFRON AND CORIANDER

⅓ cup Cognac
1 tablespoon ground coriander
½ teaspoon pulverized saffron threads
½ teaspoon salt
¼ teaspoon freshly ground black pepper
6 large whole skinless, boneless chicken breasts (about 3 pounds), split and cut into 1-inch pieces
4 tablespoons (½ stick) unsalted butter
2 tablespoons olive oil
1 can (8-ounce) tomato sauce
½ cup loosely packed fresh coriander leaves
1 pound mushrooms, cleaned and ends trimmed
1 tablespoon cornstarch or arrowroot
1 tablespoon water

In a 3-quart glass or ceramic bowl stir together the Cognac, ground coriander, saffron, salt and pepper. Add the chicken and stir to coat all the pieces. Cover with plastic wrap and let stand, at room temperature, for 1 hour, or refrigerate for up to 4 hours.

Drain the chicken, reserving the marinade, and pat dry on paper towels.

Heat 2 tablespoons of the butter with the oil in a large skillet over moderately high heat. Cook the chicken, in 2 batches, stirring constantly, until lightly browned, 2 to 3 minutes. With a slotted spoon transfer the chicken to a 4-quart saucepan. Set the skillet aside.

Add the tomato sauce and the reserved marinade to the chicken and bring to a boil over high heat. Reduce the heat to low and simmer, covered, for 8 to 10 minutes or until the chicken is tender, stirring occasionally.

While the chicken is cooking, use the metal blade of a food processor to mince the coriander leaves, processing for 10 seconds; set aside. Use the medium slicing disc to process the mushrooms; set aside. In a small bowl stir together the cornstarch and water; set aside.

Heat the remaining butter in the reserved skillet over high heat. Cook the reserved mushrooms, in 2 batches, stirring, until browned, about 3 minutes.

When the chicken is tender stir in the reserved cornstarch mixture and cook until the sauce has thickened, 1 to 2 minutes. Add the mushrooms and cook until heated through. Transfer to a serving dish and sprinkle with the reserved minced coriander.

Makes 6 to 8 servings.

PERSIAN VEGETABLE OMELET

1 cup loosely packed parsley leaves
4 medium scallions, trimmed and cut into 2-inch lengths
1 small onion, peeled and quartered
1 medium head romaine lettuce (about 10 ounces), washed and dried
8 large eggs
2 tablespoons unbleached all-purpose flour
1 teaspoon salt
½ teaspoon dried basil
½ teaspoon pulverized saffron threads
   Freshly ground black pepper
⅓ cup olive or vegetable oil

Preheat the oven to 350°F.

Use the metal blade of a food processor to mince the parsley, processing for about 15 seconds. Transfer to a 2-quart mixing bowl. Use the metal blade to process the scallions and onion, pulsing 6 to 8 times or until minced. Add to the parsley. Insert the thin slicing disc and process the romaine, standing it, tightly packed, in the feed tube. Remove to the mixing bowl.

Use the metal blade to process the eggs, flour, salt, basil, saffron and pepper to taste for 10 seconds. Add to the mixing bowl; stir thoroughly.

Heat the oil in a 10-inch ovenproof and broiler-proof skillet over moderately high heat until it is very hot. Pour in the egg and lettuce mixture, cover and place the pan in the center of the preheated oven for about 20 minutes, until the omelet is almost set. Turn on the broiler, remove the cover and place the skillet 4 to 6 inches from the heat. Cook the omelet until the top is nicely browned, about 1 minute.

Transfer to a serving dish and serve hot or at room temperature.

Makes 4 to 6 servings.

Clockwise from above:
Iced Chicken and Saffron Soup, Persian Vegetable Omelet and
Chicken in Saffron and Coriander.

It is always a pleasure to make the acquaintance of a master cook. So when Ailene Martin, a talented cooking teacher and a good friend of THE PLEASURES OF COOKING, brought Jean Berrard to our test kitchen we were delighted to welcome him. Ailene teaches in America and in France, where she met Jean. She thought, and rightly so, that we would be eager to watch him prepare a meal. As Jean began work—adjusting his fluted *toque blanche*, lining up his knives and rolling out pastry for pâté—it was apparent that he is one of that select band, the classically trained French chef.

Jean Berrard was born to his profession. From the turn of the century until very recently his family

A FRENCH CHEF COOKS DINNER

owned a hotel with restaurant in Bugey, a region of France, just east of Lyon, that is famous for its food. He spent his apprentice years under his father's guidance. This was not the usual formation for a young cook, but it was wartime and travel to other establishments was impossible. Two well-known Americans, Gertrude Stein and Alice B. Toklas, also spent the war years in Bugey, dining often at the family hotel.

The next ten years Jean spent working abroad, at

major hotel establishments such as the Mamounia in Marrakesh, the Claridge in London and the George in Edinburgh. He returned whenever possible to help his father, and succeeded him in 1955. Now retired, Jean is making his first trip to America.

As the pâté for our first course baked, Jean deftly cut the chicken into serving pieces, set it to brown and, with Ailene's able help, blanched and sautéed a cornucopia of vegetables. The dessert—almond cookies and strawberries with honey—would be prepared just before serving. As we sat down to lunch, Jean, who heeds well the precepts of that great nineteenth-century gastronome Brillat-Savarin, also from Bugey, toasted us with a glass of red wine.

Pâté Chaud

Chicken Sauté Brillat-Savarin with Prunes

Vegetable Platter

Strawberries with Honey

Almond Cookies

PATE CHAUD

You need to begin this recipe a day ahead of serving, because the meat marinates overnight.

   2 pounds boneless pork loin, trimmed
1½ pounds boneless, skinless turkey breast
   2 tablespoons sugar
   1 tablespoon salt
   1 teaspoon freshly ground white pepper
1¼ teaspoons quatre épices
   ¾ cup Madeira
      Flaky Pastry (recipe on page 36)
   1 large egg yolk
   ½ teaspoon milk
      Parsley sprigs, for garnish
      Savory Beef Sauce (recipe on page 36)

Cutting and Marinating the Meat:
Remove the tenderloin of the pork and cut it and the remaining pork lengthwise into ½-inch slices. Cut strips of meat, ½ inch wide and 3 to 6 inches long, from the slices, avoiding the fat. Cut about half of the pork into strips; set aside the rest, including the fat. Cut half of the turkey breast into strips, reserving the remainder.

Put the pork and turkey strips into a 2-quart bowl and set aside. Cut the remaining meat into 1-inch pieces and set aside in a separate 2-quart bowl.

In a small bowl stir together the sugar, salt, white pepper and quatre épices. Divide equally between the two bowls of meat and mix gently with your hands to distribute the herbs and spices evenly. Divide the Madeira equally between the two bowls; mix again.

Use the metal blade of a food processor to chop, in 2 batches, the 1-inch pieces of meat, with the marinade, to a medium coarseness, pulsing 2 or 3 times and then processing for about 15 seconds. Return to the mixing bowl. Cover both bowls loosely and set aside, at room temperature, to marinate overnight.

Assembling the Pâté:
Cut the Flaky Pastry dough crosswise into thirds. Refrigerate 2 portions. On a floured surface roll 1 portion into a rectangle about ⅛ inch thick and at least 15 by 6 inches and place it on a floured 15½- by 10½-inch baking pan. Trim the edges.

Layering the Meat:
First you will make a layer of the ground meat mixture down the center of the pastry, about 12 by 3 inches and ½ inch thick, leaving a border of pastry at least 1½ inches wide. Moisten your fingers and take about a 1-inch ball of the ground meat mixture from the bowl. Lightly flatten it between your fingers to a ½-inch thickness and place it on the dough, 1½ inches from the edge. Continue placing the flattened balls of meat on the pastry together (fig. 1, page 36) to form the first layer of ground meat. (You should use about ⅓ of the ground meat mixture.)

Then make a layer of the marinated strips of meat. Arrange them lengthwise in one layer on the ground meat, butting the strips against each other and staggering the lengths (fig. 2). (Use about ½ of the strips.)

Continue, making another ½-inch layer of the ground meat mixture, another layer of the strips and then a final layer of the ground meat.

Covering the Pâté with Pastry:
Remove a second portion of dough and, on a floured surface, roll it into a rectangle about 18 by 10 inches and about ⅛ inch thick.

Brush the bottom pastry with water around the pâté. Roll up the second portion of dough loosely on a rolling pin and carefully unroll the dough, draping it over the meat (fig. 3). Slit the top 6 or 7 times with the point of a knife. With your hands press it firmly against the sides of the pâté (fig. 4). With your index finger press it onto the bottom pastry (fig. 5). Using your finger impressions as a guide trim the pastry at the bottom, leaving about 1 inch all the way around. Then press the edges outward to flatten them and brush lightly with water. Also brush about 1 inch up the side of the pastry with water. Fold up the bottom pastry and press it against the side (fig. 6).

On a floured surface roll the remaining portion of dough to a rectangle about 18 by 10 inches and ⅛ inch thick. Brush the pâté all over with water. Roll up the dough loosely onto a rolling pin and unroll the dough, draping it over the pâté. Slit the top 6 or 7 times with the point of a knife. Press it firmly against the top and sides and then trim the edge about 1½ to 2 inches from the bottom of the pâté. Carefully tilt the pâté and tuck the pastry under it (fig. 7). At this point the pâté may be refrigerated for up to 2 days.

About 45 minutes before serving preheat the oven to 450°F.

With a fork beat together the egg yolk and milk. Brush the mixture over the top and sides of the pâté loaf. With the point of a sharp knife, make a diagonal pattern on the sides and a crisscross pattern all over the top of the loaf. Cut 3 holes, about ½ inch across, in the top of the loaf and insert paper funnels (fig. 8).

Bake in the center of the preheated oven for 30 minutes. Reduce the heat to 400°F. and bake for 10 minutes more or until the pastry is golden and the internal temperature of the pâté reaches 155° to 160°F.

Transfer to a platter and garnish with parsley. To serve, cut into ¾-inch slices with a serrated knife. Pass the Savory Beef Sauce separately.

Makes 12 to 14 servings.

Flaky Pastry

The pastry may be made up to 2 days in advance.

- 3½ cups unbleached all-purpose flour
- 2 teaspoons salt
- 20 tablespoons (2½ sticks) unsalted butter, chilled, cut into 20 pieces
- 6 tablespoons vegetable shortening, chilled
- ¼ cup ice water

Use the metal blade of a food processor to mix half of the flour and salt, processing for 2 or 3 seconds. Add half of the butter and shortening and pulse 3 or 4 times and then process for 5 seconds or until the mixture resembles coarse meal. With the machine running pour half of the ice water through the feed tube so that the mixture just holds together. Transfer to a lightly floured surface and repeat for the remaining ingredients.

Press the two batches of dough together, shape into a ball, flatten and put into a plastic storage bag. Refrigerate for about 1 hour.

On a floured surface roll the pastry into a 12-inch square. Fold it in thirds and roll again into a rectangle about 21 by 7 inches. Fold it crosswise in thirds, into a 7-inch square. Roll the dough again into a 12-inch square and fold it in thirds. Wrap in plastic and refrigerate until needed.

Makes about 3 pounds.

Savory Beef Sauce

- 9 whole cloves
- 3 medium onions, peeled
- ⅓ cup vegetable oil
- 2 pounds beef and veal bones, cut into 2-inch pieces
- 1½ pounds turkey bones, chopped into 2-inch pieces (optional)
- 2 medium ribs celery with leaves, coarsely chopped
- 2 medium carrots, coarsely chopped
- 1 large leek, thoroughly cleaned, coarsely chopped
- 6 medium garlic cloves, peeled and chopped
  Bouquet garni: 6 sprigs parsley, 1 teaspoon dried tarragon, 3 bay leaves, ½ teaspoon dried thyme leaves, ½ teaspoon dried rosemary and ½ teaspoon dried oregano tied in cheesecloth
- 2 teaspoons freshly ground white pepper
- 2 cups dry white wine
- 8 cups water

Insert the cloves into 1 of the onions in a circle at the

1. *Making the first layer with ground meat.*

2. *Making the second layer with meat strips.*

3. *Draping the second portion of dough over the pâté.*

4. *Pressing the dough against the pâté.*

5. *Pressing the dough onto the bottom pastry.*

6. *Pressing the pastry against the sides.*

7. *Tucking the third portion of dough under the pâté.*

8. *The unbaked pâté with paper funnels.*

Pâté Chaud with Savory Beef Sauce.

root end. Cut off ¼ of the top of the onion and chop it and the remaining 2 onions coarsely. Set aside.

In a large skillet, heat ¼ cup of the oil over moderately high heat. Add the bones and cook until well browned, turning occasionally, 6 to 8 minutes. With a slotted spoon remove to a 5-quart stockpot.

Add the remaining oil to the skillet, if necessary, and the celery, carrots, leek, garlic and reserved chopped onions and cook, stirring occasionally, until soft and lightly browned, about 10 minutes.

Meanwhile, put the cut end of the reserved onion with cloves directly on the burner of a stove and grill it until it is black (fig. 1). Put the grilled onion into the 5-quart stockpot. Add the bouquet garni.

When the vegetables are cooked, add the contents of the skillet and the pepper to the stockpot.

Add the wine to the skillet and stir to loosen the brown particles from the bottom. Add to the stockpot. Add the water to the stockpot.

Bring to a boil over high heat, skimming as necessary. Reduce the heat and simmer, uncovered, for 4 hours. Strain through a fine strainer into a 2-quart saucepot and skim the fat from the surface. Bring the sauce to a boil over moderately high heat and reduce to 1½ cups, about 25 minutes,

1. *Grilled onion with cloves.*

skimming occasionally. The sauce may be refrigerated for up to 2 days. To serve, reheat over low heat.

Makes about 1½ cups.

CHICKEN SAUTE BRILLAT-SAVARIN WITH PRUNES

The prunes need to soak in water overnight.

   1½ pounds large pitted prunes
    2 whole chickens (about 3 pounds each), giblets and excess fat removed
       Salt and freshly ground black pepper
   ¼ cup vegetable oil
    8 tablespoons (1 stick) unsalted butter
    6 medium shallots, peeled and coarsely chopped
    3 tablespoons unbleached all-purpose flour
    6 garlic cloves, peeled and minced
   1½ bottles dry red wine (about 38 ounces)
    1 cup water
   ⅓ cup sugar

Put the prunes in a 2-quart mixing bowl and add enough water to cover. Set aside, at room temperature, to soak overnight.

To cut each of the chickens into 8 serving pieces, remove the legs and cut them into 2 pieces at the joint. Remove the back and the wing tips at the second joint; freeze for future use. Then cut the breast in half down the length of the breast bone; cut each section in

Chicken Sauté Brillat-Savarin with Prunes and Vegetable Platter.

half crosswise. Sprinkle the chicken pieces lightly with salt and pepper.

In a large skillet heat half of the oil over moderately high heat. Add half of the chicken pieces and cook, turning occasionally, until browned on all sides, about 15 minutes. Remove and set aside. Add the remaining oil and repeat for the remaining chicken.

Meanwhile, in a 5 quart broiler-proof casserole melt the butter over moderate heat. Add the shallots and cook, stirring occasionally, until browned, about 5 minutes. Remove from the heat.

Preheat the broiler.

Transfer the browned chicken pieces to the casserole. Sprinkle the flour over the chicken pieces and put under the broiler until the flour has browned slightly, about 6 to 8 minutes. Remove and set aside.

Discard all but 1 teaspoon of fat from the skillet.

With the side of a large heavy knife mash the minced garlic to a puree. Add to the skillet and cook over moderately high heat for about 1 minute. Add 1 bottle (about 3 cups) of the red wine and bring to a boil, stirring to release all of the brown bits from the bottom of the skillet. Add the water and boil the mixture until reduced to about 3 cups, about 20 minutes.

Pour the reduced liquid over the reserved chicken, stir well and simmer, covered, over moderately low heat for about 20 minutes or until the chicken is done.

Meanwhile, in a 2-quart saucepan over moderate heat stir together the remaining wine and the sugar until the sugar has dissolved. Drain the prunes and add them to the saucepan. Reduce the heat slightly, cover and simmer for 15 to 20 minutes. Transfer the prunes and their liquid to a serving bowl. Serve the chicken from the casserole and present the prunes separately.

Makes 8 servings.

VEGETABLE PLATTER

Choose seasonal vegetables according to your preference. The vegetables may be blanched 2 to 3 hours ahead; they should be cooked in butter just before serving.

> Vegetables in season, trimmed, cleaned and cut into serving-size pieces
> Unsalted butter
> Salt and freshly ground black pepper
> Fresh lemon juice (optional)

Blanch the vegetables, if necessary, separately in lightly salted boiling water until barely tender (mushrooms, for example, need not be blanched). Drain, refresh under cold running water and set aside.

Shortly before serving, for each vegetable, heat 1 to 2 tablespoons of butter in a medium skillet over moderate heat. Add the vegetable and cook, stirring often, until heated through.

STRAWBERRIES WITH HONEY

> 3 pints strawberries, hulled
> 1 cup honey
> 1 cup heavy cream, chilled
> 2 tablespoons confectioners' sugar
> 1 teaspoon pure vanilla extract
> ¼ cup finely chopped fresh mint leaves
> 1 tablespoon grated lemon peel
>   Strips of lemon peel, for garnish

Arrange the strawberries in a shallow serving dish or in individual dishes. Set aside.

In a 1-quart saucepan over moderate heat bring the honey to a boil. Reduce the heat and simmer until the honey has thickened and turned a deep amber, about 10 minutes.

Meanwhile, in a 2-quart bowl beat the cream until it just begins to hold its shape. Sift the confectioners' sugar over the top and continue to beat until stiff peaks form. Stir in the vanilla. Refrigerate until needed.

To serve, spoon the hot honey over the strawberries. Sprinkle with the mint and grated lemon peel. Garnish with the whipped cream and strips of lemon peel.

Makes 8 servings.

ALMOND COOKIES

> 7 tablespoons sugar
> 3 egg whites
> ½ cup blanched almonds
> ⅓ cup cake flour
> 1 teaspoon Cointreau or Grand Marnier liqueur
> ¼ teaspoon pure vanilla extract

In a 1-quart mixing bowl stir together the sugar and egg whites. Set aside at room temperature for 1 hour.

Use the metal blade of a food processor to chop the almonds finely, processing for about 45 seconds. Add to the egg white mixture. Add the cake flour, Cointreau and vanilla and stir thoroughly.

Preheat the oven to 425°F. Oil well two 17- by 14-inch baking sheets.

Drop the batter, ½ rounded teaspoon at a time, onto the baking sheet, leaving 2 to 3 inches between the cookies. Bake in the preheated oven for 5 to 6 minutes or until the edge of the cookies are lightly browned. Remove to a wire rack to cool completely.

Makes about 6½ dozen.

Strawberries with Honey and Almond Cookies.

GUATEMALAN BRUNCH

by Copeland Marks

Curious as it may seem, the cooking of Guatemala's highland country admirably suits that all–American institution, a brunch party. Those who appreciate such staples of Mexican cuisine as beans and tortillas will find them in a different guise in Guatemalan cuisine.

Most of the basic ingredients found in Guatemalan cooking are familiar: tomatoes, sweet red peppers, corn. Queso blanco (white cheese) is very much like our farmer cheese. Mexican and Guatemalan foods emerged from a common botanical heritage, so it is logical to look for such Guatemalan staples as achiote (the red seed of the annatto tree that colors foods) and black beans in a market stocking Mexican foods. Remember, however, that Guatemalan and Mexican cooking differs.

Almost all of the recipes presented here may be prepared completely or partly the day before the brunch party. The dishes complement one another harmoniously, and for the true savor of Guatemala, I urge you to serve them all at one time.

GRAPEFRUIT MEDLEY
Pico de Gallo

- 3 large grapefruits
- 1 small sweet red pepper, cored, seeded and cut into ¼-inch dice
- 2 tablespoons minced parsley
- 2 teaspoons minced onion
- ½ teaspoon crushed red pepper
- ½ teaspoon salt

With a serrated knife peel the grapefruits, taking care to remove all of the white pith. With a small sharp

knife cut out the grapefruit segments, discarding the membranes.

Cut the segments into ½-inch pieces and put them into a 2-quart bowl. Add the remaining ingredients. Stir gently to mix. Refrigerate for at least 1 hour before serving.

Makes 6 to 8 servings.

RED SAUSAGE PATTIES
Chorizo

½ teaspoon achiote paste or 1 tablespoon achiote seeds (see NOTE, follows)
1 teaspoon warm water
2 small garlic cloves, peeled
1 pound boneless pork shoulder, cut into 1-inch cubes, chilled
1 teaspoon salt
½ teaspoon ground cumin
½ teaspoon dried oregano leaves
½ teaspoon freshly ground black pepper
2 tablespoons vegetable oil

Stir the achiote paste into the water until dissolved; set aside.

Use the metal blade of a food processor and, with the machine running, drop 1 of the garlic cloves through the feed tube and process until minced. Scrape down the bowl. Add half of the pork cubes and pulse 12 to 14 times or until finely chopped. Set aside. Repeat for the remaining garlic and pork cubes. Add the salt, cumin, oregano, pepper, reserved achiote mixture and reserved pork mixture to the food processor bowl and pulse 4 to 6 times or until well mixed. Shape into 3-inch patties, about ¼ inch thick.

In a large skillet heat the oil over moderately high heat. Cook the patties, without crowding, until browned and cooked through, about 3 minutes on each side. Drain on paper towels.

Makes about 8 sausage patties.

NOTE: To use achiote seeds instead of paste, heat 2 tablespoons of vegetable oil in a small saucepan. Add 1 tablespoon achiote seeds and stir over low heat for about 1½ minutes or until the oil is dark red. Strain and use in place of the achiote paste mixture.

SPICED SAUSAGE PATTIES
Longanizo

2 tablespoons chopped onion
2 tablespoons parsley leaves
2 tablespoons orange juice
1 tablespoon apple cider vinegar
1 teaspoon salt
½ teaspoon sugar

½ teaspoon freshly ground black pepper
1 pound boneless pork shoulder, cut into 1-inch cubes, chilled
1 tablespoon vegetable oil

Use the metal blade of a food processor and, with the machine running, drop the onion and parsley through the feed tube and process until minced. Scrape down the bowl, add the orange juice, vinegar, salt, sugar and pepper and process until combined, about 10 seconds. Set aside in a 2-quart mixing bowl. Process half of the pork cubes until finely chopped, pulsing 12 to 14 times. Add to the mixing bowl. Process the remaining pork until finely chopped. Return all of the pork and reserved seasoning to the food processor bowl and pulse 4 to 6 times or until well mixed. Shape into 2-inch patties, about ¼ inch thick.

In a large skillet heat the oil over moderate heat. Cook the sausage patties, without crowding, until browned and cooked through, about 3 minutes on each side. Drain on paper towels.

Makes about 16 sausage patties.

KERNEL CORN PANCAKES
Tortillas de Elote

¼ cup milk
1 stick (2-inch) cinnamon
2 tablespoons unsalted butter
2 tablespoons sugar
1 can (12-ounce) whole kernel corn, drained
3 tablespoons unbleached all-purpose flour
1 large egg
Vegetable oil for frying
1 cup honey, warmed

Put the milk and cinnamon stick in a 1-quart saucepan and bring to a boil over moderate heat. Reduce the heat and simmer for 10 minutes. Add the butter and sugar and stir until the butter has melted. Remove from the heat and let stand for 10 minutes. Remove and discard the cinnamon stick.

Use the metal blade of a food processor to puree the corn, about 1½ minutes, stopping once to scrape the bowl. Add the flour, egg and reserved milk mixture; process for 10 seconds more. Set aside, covered, for at least 20 minutes.

Preheat the oven to its lowest setting. Line a baking sheet with a double layer of paper towels and set aside.

Stir the batter. Pour a thin film of oil into a medium skillet and heat over moderate heat. Drop the batter by tablespoons into the skillet, without crowding the pancakes. Cook for 1½ to 2 minutes or until the bottoms are brown and the tops have begun to dry. Carefully turn the pancakes and cook for about 2

*A Gathering of Guatemalan Delights.
Clockwise from below: Fried Black Bean Roll, Grapefruit
Medley, a serving of Kernel Corn Pancakes, Spiced
Sausage Patties and Stuffed Baked Tortillas with
Chirmol Sauce—another serving of tortillas
and pancakes with Red Sausage Patties—
Banana and Orange Jam, and
Coconut Milk Rolls.*

minutes more, until browned. Remove to the prepared baking sheet and keep warm in the preheated oven. Repeat for the remaining batter, adding oil to the skillet as necessary.

Serve with the warm honey.

Makes about 16 pancakes.

BAKED STUFFED TORTILLAS
Chilaquilas

  1 small onion, peeled and quartered
  1 small sweet red pepper, cored, seeded and cut into 1-inch pieces
12 ounces (1½ cups) farmer cheese, cut into 6 pieces, at room temperature
  ½ teaspoon freshly ground black pepper
  4 large eggs, separated
  1 teaspoon unbleached all-purpose flour
  ¼ teaspoon salt
12 corn tortillas
  ¼ cup vegetable oil
    Chirmol Sauce (recipe follows)
  2 tablespoons minced fresh cilantro, for garnish

Use the metal blade of a food processor to chop the onion coarsely, pulsing 4 to 6 times. Add the red pepper and pulse 3 or 4 times or until chopped to a medium coarseness. Add the farmer cheese and pepper and pulse 10 to 12 times to mix. Set aside.

In a small bowl beat the egg yolks lightly with a fork. Add the flour and beat until blended. Set aside.

With a wire whisk or an electric mixer beat the egg whites with the salt until stiff peaks form. Gently fold in the reserved egg yolk mixture. Set aside.

Preheat the oven to 350°F.

Place 2 to 3 tablespoons of the reserved cheese mixture in the center of each tortilla and fold in half. (Do not worry if the tortillas crack.) Set aside.

In a large skillet heat the oil over moderate heat. Dip the filled tortillas in the reserved egg batter and with a table knife spread the batter evenly over them. Cook a few at a time, without crowding, in the hot oil until lightly browned, about 1 minute on each side. Remove to paper towels to drain. Repeat for the remaining tortillas.

In a 13- by 9- by 2-inch baking dish, arrange the fried tortillas, overlapping, in a row. Spoon about ¾ cup of the Chirmol Sauce in a strip down the center and bake in the preheated oven for about 20 minutes or until slightly crisp.

Just before serving, heat the remaining Chirmol Sauce over low heat. Garnish the baked tortillas with the minced cilantro and serve with the warm sauce.

Makes 6 to 8 servings.

Chirmol Sauce

1 medium garlic clove, peeled
1 small onion, peeled and quartered
1 can (28-ounce) Italian peeled tomatoes, drained
¼ cup water
¼ teaspoon salt
¼ teaspoon sugar

Use the metal blade of a food processor and, with the machine running, drop the garlic through the feed tube and process until minced. Add the onion and pulse 4 to 6 times to chop it coarsely. Add the tomatoes and pulse 2 or 3 times or until coarsely chopped. Add the water, salt and sugar and pulse 2 or 3 times to mix. Transfer the mixture to a small saucepan and simmer over moderately low heat for 10 minutes.

Return the mixture to the food processor bowl and use the metal blade to process until smooth, about 10 seconds. Return to the saucepan and simmer over moderately low heat for 5 to 10 minutes or until the sauce has thickened slightly and is no longer watery.

Makes about 2 cups.

FRIED BLACK BEAN ROLL
Frijoles Negros Volteados

  2 cups dried black beans (turtle beans), rinsed and picked over
  4 cups water
  ¼ cup chopped onion
  2 medium garlic cloves, peeled and coarsely chopped
1½ teaspoons salt
  3 tablespoons vegetable oil
  8 ounces imported feta cheese or mozzarella cheese, cut into ½-inch cubes (about 1½ cups)

Put the beans in a 4-quart saucepan. Add the water and set aside to soak overnight.

The next day, add the onion, garlic and salt to the saucepan. If all of the water has been absorbed, add another 1 cup of water. Bring to a boil over moderate heat. Lower the heat, cover and simmer for about 45 minutes or until the beans are very soft and some liquid remains. If at any time the beans begin to stick to the bottom of the pan, add about ¼ cup of water.

Use the metal blade of a food processor to puree the bean mixture, in 2 batches, processing for about 30 seconds and stopping once or twice to scrape the bowl.

In a medium skillet heat the oil over moderately low heat. Add the bean puree and stir constantly with a wooden spoon until the moisture has evaporated, about 20 minutes.

Then begin to shake the skillet back and forth on the burner. As the puree starts to dry out it will draw away from the side of the skillet. Continue to shake the pan. As the puree becomes dryer and firmer, gradually push it toward the center of the skillet with a spatula and form it into a cylindrical roll about 8 inches long. The shaping process will take about 5 minutes.

Slide the roll onto a serving dish, surround with the cheese cubes and serve.

Makes 6 to 8 servings.

COCONUT MILK ROLLS
Pan de Coco

  1 package dry yeast
  1 teaspoon sugar
  1 cup Rich Coconut Milk (recipe follows), heated
     to 105° to 115°F.
  3 cups unbleached all-purpose flour
  ¼ teaspoon salt
  2 tablespoons vegetable oil

Stir the yeast and sugar into the warm coconut milk. Set aside for 10 minutes.

Use the metal blade of a food processor to mix the flour and salt, processing for about 5 seconds. With the machine running, pour the yeast mixture and the oil through the feed tube in a steady stream. Process until the dough forms a ball and cleans the side of the bowl; then process for 45 seconds more to knead the dough. (If the mixture is too dry to form a ball, add water or coconut milk by teaspoons with the machine running; if the dough is too sticky to clean the side of the bowl, add flour by tablespoons with the machine running.)

Remove the dough to a lightly oiled 3-quart mixing bowl and cover with oiled plastic wrap. Set aside in a warm place (75° to 80°F.) to rise until doubled in volume, about 45 minutes.

Punch down the dough and transfer it to a smooth surface. Shape it into a cylinder about 10 inches long and 2 inches in diameter. Cut the cylinder crosswise into 8 equal pieces. Roll each piece into a ball. Flatten the balls slightly and place them on an ungreased 17- by 14-inch baking sheet, about 3 inches apart.

Cover and set aside to rise until almost doubled in volume, about 40 minutes.

Preheat the oven to 375°F.

Bake the rolls in the center of the preheated oven for about 25 minutes or until golden brown.

Makes 8 rolls.

Rich Coconut Milk

  1 fresh coconut (about 3 pounds)
  3 cups hot tap water

Preheat the oven to 400°F. Bake the whole coconut, in a baking pan, until the shell cracks, about 15 minutes. Remove to a rack until the coconut is cool enough to handle.

Put the coconut inside two plastic bags and seal them with a wire twist. With a hammer, hit the coconut solidly where the shell is cracked; one or two blows should split it open.

Discard the coconut liquid and carefully separate the meat from the shell with a small paring knife. With a swivel-bladed vegetable peeler, remove the brown skin from the coconut meat. Cut the meat into 1-inch pieces.

Use the metal blade of a food processor to process half the coconut, pulsing 10 times or until coarsely chopped. With the machine running pour 1½ cups of the hot water through the feed tube. Continue to process for 1 minute. Pour the pureed coconut mixture into a 2-quart mixing bowl. Repeat with the remaining coconut and hot water. Let stand for 15 minutes.

Strain the mixture through a colander lined with rinsed cheesecloth, pressing down on the coconut to extract as much liquid as possible. Discard the solids. Let the liquid stand for 10 minutes. Then carefully pour off the milk into another container discarding the sediment. The milk may be refrigerated in an airtight container for up to 2 days or frozen for up to 2 months.

Makes about 3 cups.

BANANA AND ORANGE JAM
Jalea de Banana

  3 large ripe bananas (about 1 pound), peeled and
     cut into 1-inch pieces
  4 cups orange juice
  3 cups sugar

Use the metal blade of a food processor to process the bananas to a coarse puree, about 20 seconds. Transfer to a 4-quart saucepan. Whisk in the orange juice and sugar.

Boil the mixture over moderate heat for about 45 minutes or until it has thickened and reaches a temperature of 240°F. (A few drops of the jam dropped into a glass of cold water should just hold together.)

Skim off the foam and pour into glass jars. Set aside to cool; then cover and refrigerate for up to 1 month.

Makes about 3½ cups.

HOMEMADE DOUBLE CHOCOLATE PUDDING

Nearly everyone has a favorite chocolate mousse recipe, but when was the last time you had a real homemade chocolate pudding?

      2¼ cups milk
      ½ cup sugar
         Pinch salt
      2 tablespoons cornstarch, sifted
      3 tablespoons Dutch cocoa
      1 egg
      2 egg yolks
      5 ounces semisweet chocolate, preferably imported, cut up
      2 tablespoons unsalted butter
      1 teaspoon pure vanilla extract
         Lightly whipped cream

Heat 2 cups of the milk, ¼ cup of the sugar, and salt in heavy saucepan over medium heat to boiling.

Mix together cornstarch, cocoa, and the remaining ¼ cup of the sugar in a bowl.

Whisk the remaining ¼ cup of the milk into the dry ingredients until smooth and thoroughly blended. Slowly whisk in the hot milk mixture; return to saucepan. Slowly bring to the boil over medium heat, stirring constantly. Gently boil 2 minutes, stirring constantly; the mixture should become fairly thick.

Whisk egg and yolks together in small bowl. Slowly whisk in 1 cup of cocoa mixture. Whisk back into cocoa-cornstarch mixture. Cook, whisking constantly, over low to medium heat, about 2 minutes, until mixture becomes slightly thicker. Do not allow the mixture to boil or overcook. Transfer to clean bowl and lay a sheet of waxed paper directly on surface. Cool slightly on wire rack.

Melt semisweet chocolate in top of double boiler over simmering water. Blend in the butter. Cool slightly; chocolate should remain pourable.

Whisk chocolate into thickened egg mixture. Stir in vanilla. Cool pudding in bowl on wire rack. Refrigerate. Serve chilled with lightly whipped cream. Serves 4.

ALMOND BRITTLE COOKIES

         Unsalted butter for baking pan
      1 recipe Cookie Crust (recipe follows)
      ½ cup jam, such as raspberry, black currant or apricot
      1½ tablespoons brandy or liqueur (optional)
      9 tablespoons (½ cup plus 1 tablespoon) unsalted butter

"Cooking Great Meals Every Day" by Richard Sax in collaboration with David Ricketts, Random House, 1982 ($15.95 hard cover)
Copyright © 1982 by Richard Sax and David Ricketts

If one thinks of great meals as memorable and complicated haute cuisine, the title of Richard Sax's book may be misleading; however, if delicious home cooking from carefully written recipes is your wish, you will appreciate this book. "My aim is to take the good food I've learned working with chefs in Europe and to translate it into manageable terms," says Richard. "I use ingredients that are easy to get without compromising quality."

Richard considers himself to be a generalist in his approach to cooking, but confesses to a great love for desserts. We present two from his book: satisfying Almond Brittle Cookies and an exceedingly rich Homemade Double Chocolate Pudding.

9 tablespoons (½ cup plus 1 tablespoon) sugar
¼ teaspoon salt
2 heaping tablespoons honey
¼ cup heavy cream
1 teaspoon pure vanilla extract
  Few drops fresh lemon juice
2 cups sliced blanched almonds (6 ounces)

Lightly butter 15½ x 10½ x 1-inch baking pan. Roll out dough slightly larger than pan. Carefully transfer dough to pan, allowing rough edges to hang over sides of pan. Chill for 20 minutes or more.

Preheat oven to 400°F.

Trim edges of dough flush with outside edges of pan. Prick dough all over with fork. Bake until just lightly golden, 14 to 18 minutes, pricking any bubbles with a fork as they rise. Do not overbake as pastry will be baked a second time. Cool pastry slightly.

In a small cup or bowl, stir together jam and optional liqueur. Brush or spoon a thin layer of jam over pastry.

For the remainder of the topping, melt the 9 tablespoons butter in heavy saucepan. Add sugar, salt, and honey; cook over low heat, stirring, until sugar dissolves. Increase heat to medium. Add cream; boil, stirring, until mixture is smooth and thickened. Remove from heat; add vanilla, lemon juice, and almonds. Stir. Gently spread a smooth layer over pastry. Bake until bubbly and golden brown, 12 to 20 minutes.

Cool thoroughly on wire rack. Cut into 1½-inch squares; trim rough edges and save for snacking.

Makes about 6 dozen.

Cookie Crust

This recipe belongs to a wonderful Italian baker named Carlo Bussetti. Makes one 10½ x 15½-inch sheet, or two 10-inch tart shells.

2 sticks (8 ounces) unsalted butter
1 cup sugar
  Pinch of salt
  Grated zest of 2 oranges
¼ cup lightly beaten egg (1 extra-large egg, or 1 large egg plus 1 yolk)
2 tablespoons milk
2 teaspoons pure vanilla extract
2 cups cake flour (6 ounces)
1½ cups all-purpose flour (6 ounces)

Cream butter with electric mixer. Add sugar, salt, and grated orange zest; beat until fluffy. Beat in egg, milk, and vanilla. Lower mixer speed; add flours. Stop mixing as soon as flour is mixed in. Do not overmix or dough will be tough. Dough should be soft, but not sticky. Gather dough together. Dust with flour; wrap, and chill well. Let dough soften briefly before rolling out.

Food Processor Method

Use the metal blade of a food processor to mince the orange zest with the sugar, processing for 1 minute or until the zest is finely minced. Cut the butter into 16 pieces. Add the butter and process until smooth, about 10 seconds. Add the egg, milk, salt and vanilla and pulse 4 to 6 times and process 5 seconds or until smooth. Add the flours and process for 5 seconds. Scrape down the bowl and process 5 seconds more or just until the flour is incorporated. Do not overprocess. Gather dough together. Dust with flour; wrap and chill well. Let dough soften briefly before rolling out.

Almond Brittle Cookies, below, and Home-made Double Chocolate Pudding.

Sharing Recipes

Amy Dee Shaftel will be graduating from Oberlin College this June. She spent last year studying at the Sorbonne, in Paris, refining her French. In her spare time there, she improved her cooking skills. "France is a wonderful place to learn classical cooking techniques," she says, "but here in America I love to experiment on my own."

Amy adapted a recipe for lemon tart, using the rind and juice of a lime instead of a lemon. We think her Lime Almond Tart is a great success—and that Amy is ready for graduate cooking school.

LIME ALMOND TART

    9-inch partially baked Tart Shell (recipe follows)
  ½ cup plus 1 tablespoon slivered blanched almonds
  2 large limes
  ½ cup sugar
  2 large eggs
  6 tablespoons (¾ stick) unsalted butter, melted
  1 cup heavy cream, whipped

Use the metal blade of a food processor to chop ½ cup of almonds finely. Set aside. Preheat the oven to 350°F.

With a vegetable peeler remove the rind from 1 of the limes. Squeeze both limes; reserve 3 tablespoons of juice.

Use the metal blade to chop the rind with the sugar, pulsing 3 or 4 times and then processing until the rind is finely chopped, about 2 minutes. Add the eggs, butter, reserved ground almonds and lime juice and pulse 2 or 3 times and then process 8 to 10 seconds until well mixed, stopping once to scrape the bowl.

Fill the tart shell with the almond mixture and bake on a baking sheet in the center of the preheated oven for 20 to 25 minutes or until the top is lightly browned. Remove to a wire rack to cool completely. Meanwhile, put the remaining almonds on a baking sheet and toast in the preheated oven for 5 to 8 minutes; set aside.

Remove the side of the tart pan and slide the tart onto a serving dish. Garnish with half of the whipped cream and reserved toasted almonds. Serve with the remaining whipped cream.

Makes 8 servings.

Tart Shell

  1½ cups unbleached all-purpose flour
    8 tablespoons (1 stick) unsalted butter, chilled and cut into 8 pieces
  2 teaspoons sugar
    Pinch of salt
  1 large egg yolk
  1 tablespoon ice water

Use the metal blade of a food processor to process the flour, butter, sugar and salt, pulsing 2 or 3 times and then processing for 8 seconds or until the mixture resembles coarse meal. With the machine running pour the egg yolk and water through the feed tube and process just until the dough begins to come together. (If the dough does not come together, add water by teaspoons until it does.) Transfer to a lightly floured surface and form the dough into a ball. Then flatten it into a disc, wrap in plastic wrap and refrigerate for 30 minutes. Preheat the oven to 400°F.

On a lightly floured surface roll the chilled dough into an 11-inch circle and transfer it to a 9-inch tart pan with a removable bottom, pressing the dough gently against the bottom and side taking care not to stretch the dough. Press the dough into a rim and remove the excess dough. Prick the bottom with a fork. Line the shell with parchment paper or aluminum foil and fill with dried beans. Place the pan on a baking sheet and bake in the center of the preheated oven for 15 minutes. Remove the paper and beans and return to the oven for 5 to 10 minutes more or until the pastry is set but not browned. Remove the pan to a wire rack until needed.

RSVP

We invite our readers to share their favorite recipes. If yours is a family recipe, we'd enjoy knowing its background. If it comes from a cookbook, let us know which one; also whether you have adapted it and how. As a token of our appreciation, if we publish your recipe we will send you three current cookbooks of your choice. Address: Sharing Recipes, THE PLEASURES OF COOKING, 411 West Putnam Avenue, Greenwich, Connecticut 06830.

Lime Almond T...

Recipe Index

"Cleo White" china plate on our cover and on pages 2, 3 and 7 courtesy of Haviland & Co., 11 East 26th Street, N.Y., N.Y. 10010.

Plates on pages 11 and 13 courtesy of The Lee Bailey at Henri Bendel, 10 West 57th Street, N.Y., N.Y. 10019.

Glass salad bowl on page 14 and sterling silver cake knife on page 22 courtesy of Rita Sacks, Manhattan Art & Antiques Center, 1050 Second Avenue, N.Y., N.Y.; "Vieux Paris" china on pages 14, 15 and 22 courtesy of Haviland & Co.; silver platter on page 22 courtesy of Tibor's Antiques, 1050 Second Avenue, N.Y., N.Y. 10022; champagne glasses on page 22 courtesy of The Pottery Barn, 231 Tenth Avenue, N.Y., N.Y. 10011.

Delft scale, lower left on page 24, courtesy of Rita Sacks.

Glasses on page 40, 42 and 43, silver ladle on page 42, glass bowl holding honey, designed by Simon Pearce, on page 43 and plates on pages 42 and 43 courtesy of Frank McIntosh at Henri Bendel, 10 West 57th Street, N.Y., N.Y. 10019.

From the slender threads found within the blue flower of
Crocus sativus *come the world's costliest spice: saffron. For*
an array of recipes in which saffron is judiciously used, see
"A Touch of Saffron," page 27.